Dear Niel
Keep the rubberside down!
Awesome to see you again in [illegible]
SUSIE [illegible]

Keep the shiny side up ↑↑!
old MTBikers never die -
they just go downhill faster!
Herman Mills Aug 2013

BEST MOUNTAIN BIKE RIDES
IN SOUTH AFRICA

JACQUES MARAIS
SUSANNA & HERMAN MILLS

BEST MOUNTAIN BIKE RIDES IN SOUTH AFRICA

JACQUES MARAIS
SUSANNA & HERMAN MILLS

First published in 2004 by Struik Publishers
(a division of New Holland Publishing (South Africa) (Pty) Ltd)
New Holland Publishing is a member of Johnnic Communications Ltd
Log on to our photographic website www.imagesofafrica.co.za

Garfield House, 86–88 Edgware Road, London W2 2EA, United Kingdom, www.newhollandpublishers.com
80 McKenzie Street, Cape Town 8001, South Africa, www.struik.co.za
14 Aquatic Drive, Frenchs Forest, NSW 2086, Australia
218 Lake Road, Northcote, Auckland, New Zealand

ISBN 1 86872 825 0
1 3 5 7 9 10 8 6 4 2

Publishing manager: Dominique le Roux
Managing editor: Lesley Hay-Whitton
Editor: Erika Bornman
Designer: Alison Day
Proofreader: Tessa Kennedy
Indexer: Mary Lennox

Reproduction by Hirt & Carter Cape (Pty) Ltd
Printed and bound by Sing Cheong Printing Company Limited

DISCLAIMER

While every effort has been made to ensure accuracy, the authors and the publisher will not be liable for any inconvenience or loss resulting from possible inaccuracies. Information such as telephone numbers, email addresses, roads and maps could have changed since the authors researched the routes, and the publisher would appreciate updated information. Please write to: The Editor, *Best Mountain Bike Rides in South Africa*, PO Box 1144, Cape Town, 8000 or email updates@struik.co.za

FRONT COVER: Overlooking False Bay near Miller's Point, Simon's Town.
HALF-TITLE PAGE: Sandstone balancing in the Cederberg.
PREVIOUS PAGE: Riding on the cliffs near Coffee Bay, Wild Coast.
OPPOSITE: Sandstone formations near Lot's Wife in the Cederberg.
FOLLOWING PAGE: Riding on granite rocks in the Richtersveld.
BACK COVER: Water crossing at Eselfontein farm in the Western Cape.

CONTENTS

HOW TO...

BEST MOUNTAIN BIKE RIDES IN SA

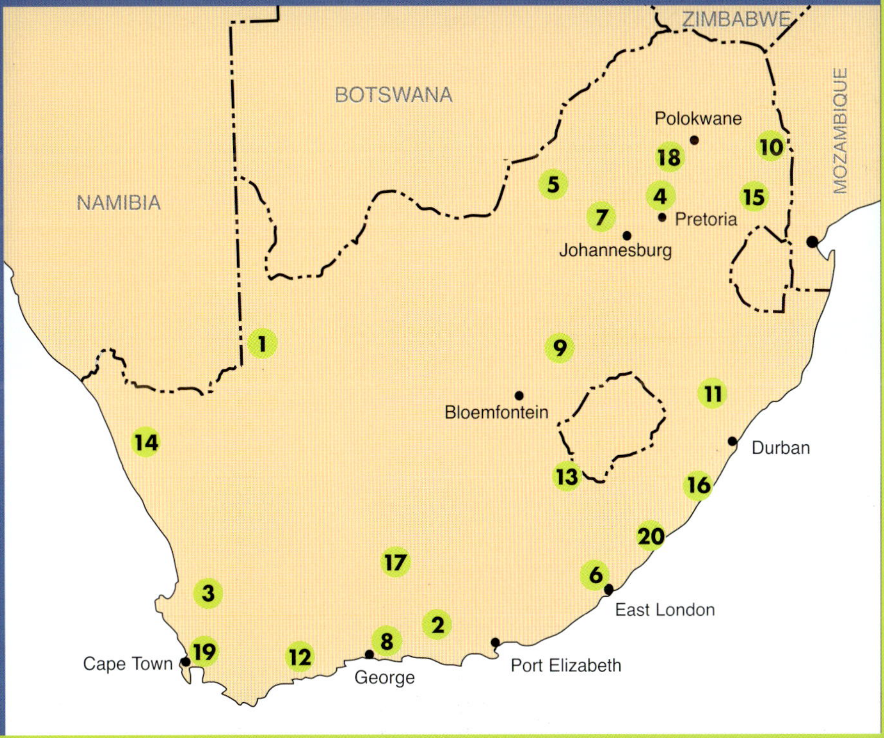

The tribe has gathered. Knobblies rule as far as the eye can see, bristling black upon mean downhill bombers and racy cross-country machines. Trail bikes, BMXs, mini bicycles with training wheels and the odd dainty pink number boasting a white basket whiz in and out of the mix. Smoke from braai fires drifts upon the afternoon breeze, swirling amidst a tent town that has mushroomed on the slopes of the Sonderend Mountains. You've guessed it – it's Easter and the annual Dirtopia Mountain Bike Festival.

For a few days, wiry enduro riders, youthful downhill chargers, big air dirt merchants and foot-up renegades share the mountain bike stage with XC athletes, teenie dual artistes, recreational riders and your common or garden variety weekend warrior. Father and daughter teams take on the challenge of mountain biking orienteering; moms strut their stuff during XC lap racing; greybeards kick butt in the enduro and boys become men amidst the rough and tumble of the dual course.

That Easter mountain bike fest represents everything we love about mountain biking. This book is about capturing this spirit and extending it across some of the greatest trails this country has to offer, all year round. More than most other sports, mountain biking crosses over a great number of social and cultural divides to embrace participation from all walks of life. Age, sex, race, financial status and competency are largely irrelevant – as long as you have enough love for riding coursing through your veins. At the end of the day, riding your bike is not about winning races, but rather about riding to the best of your own ability and relishing every minute on the bike.

Welcome to the clan – now go out and enjoy your ride!

Jacques Marais

Susanna and Herman Mills

South Africa's favourite mountain bike trails led us to travel all over the country and ride in amazing places with our mates. The views across the bars, the crunch of gravel beneath our wheels and those late night campfire stories are what real life should be all about.

Problem is, within a country featuring as many diverse riding options as South Africa, you are bound to miss out on some great rides along the way. This, therefore, became the most difficult aspect of the book: how does one select twenty riding regions within a country encompassing the full gamut from dramatic mountain deserts to temperate forests and tropical coastlines? At the end of the day, we tried our damnedest to locate at least one ride within easy reach of every rider in the country.

While Jacques Marais focused on the Western, Eastern and Northern Cape, Susie and Herman Mills teamed up to cover the north-eastern regions. Between us, we wanted to feature a selection of rides achievable by anyone from rookie riders to the 'hardebaard' heroes out there. The highlighted routes are therefore not necessarily all hardcore trails, but rather enjoyable routes allowing you to explore some of the most beautiful parts of our country while riding your bike.

Every chapter in this book focuses on a flagship trail set within an exceptional off-road riding region and key to this is 'Best ride', a no-holds-barred description of the route, crank by delectable crank, from start to finish. Distances, hazards and directional info are based upon our own riding experiences along these routes, so expect a dollop of personal opinion along the way. Additional to this, you will find out when the best time is to go, how to get there and what to expect when you arrive, plus tips and techniques that will help you cope with terrain conditions along the various rides.

Map graphics and altitude profiles accompany each of the flagship rides, and these have been mapped using Garmin GPS technology. Forest rides such as Hogsback and Harkerville posed problems in this regard, with sections of the ride so dense it was impossible to track via satellite. We have done our utmost to ensure exact information, but in the above cases it will obviously be impossible to guarantee we are 100% correct with regard to distance and altitude.

Each ride also features a grading diagram and this is an essential tool. The difficulty rating varies between easy, moderate, difficult and extreme, with this rating based on various factors. These factors are distance, time in the saddle, danger (this is a rather subjective area, but we attempted to look at terrain factors, some that might well lead to serious injury along the route), technical level (rated according to how rideable the overall route surface is for the average rider) and gradient.

The Regions

Western Cape

Nowhere else in our country will you get more ride for your rand than in the sprawling Western Cape region. Five of our featured flagship rides are set in the province: the Tokai singletrack on the Peninsula, Grootvadersbosch in the Overberg, a sandstone trail through the Cederberg, a tortuous climb into the menacing Swartberg ranges and the unrivalled Harkerville ride near Knysna. Two regions not included in this book but deserving of special mention are Ceres (specifically Eselfontein Farm with its glorious fynbos singletrack) and Montagu, a country dorp with a superb selection of off-road routes.

Eastern Cape

Diverse riding is the name of the game in the Eastern Cape and the four featured rides in this province will take you to dense forest (Hogsback), the subalpine landscape of the southern Drakensberg (Rhodes), arid thornveld savanna (Baviaans River Conservancy) and a breathtaking subtropical coastline (Wild Coast). Riding within this heartland of the amaXhosa will transport you beyond well-marked routes and cell phone reception into the domain of full-on MTB adventure, so be prepared.

Northern Cape

Although the barren plains and mountainous desert of the Northern Cape are not normally associated with mountain biking, this region boasts several superb riding spots. Augrabies National Park rates as one of my favourite gravel game rides, while the Richtersveld will test your cycling skills to the limit.

Gauteng

Home to the majority of the country's cyclists, Gauteng, the smallest and most dynamic province in South Africa, is losing its natural areas piece by piece to urbanisation. Those who foresaw this unbridled development have conserved a few pockets of nature where it is still possible to be a mountain biking purist. Hemmed in by the skyscrapers, freeways and historical monuments of Pretoria (Tshwane) lies Fountains Valley, a green gem of inestimable value that is being rehabilitated to its original natural glory by 'the garden city' authorities. We chose Groenkloof Nature Reserve for its delightful close-up encounters with non-predatory African game and the peace of mind afforded by controlled access to the reserve. Ingwe Bush Camp, nestling against the Magaliesberg massif in the shadow of Nooitgedacht, was our next choice for its historical significance, mystic beauty and the affordability of its tented camp experience. Nooitgedacht, the very highest point of the Magaliesberg, is visible from the northwestern suburbs of Johannesburg, a highly accessible, 45-minute drive away.

North West Province

This large, rural province, bordering on Botswana, still remains largely undiscovered. The long-time locals of Groot Marico told us how this area was even overlooked by engineers of the infamous 1946 Group Areas Act, resulting in a very rare Indian community that has roots way back in the 1800s. This uniqueness extends into the absolute Eden that off-road cyclists can experience. Tough and definitely for the more adventurous, riding here is a heady mix of pushing back frontiers and the clock. It simply will not fail to make a deposit into your spiritual bank account.

KwaZulu-Natal

Legions of ride options exist in this very scenic province, but local riders remain tight-lipped since there are regrettably very few rides they do that are 'legal'. The official on-again-off-again status of mountain biking in this province led to Mike's Pass, a stunning ride in Cathedral Peak, being omitted. Consequently, we 'discovered' KZN Wildlife's lovely Vernon Crookes Nature Reserve in Umzinto, slightly inland, on the South Coast. And the Midlands Meander has certainly come of age in terms of making the journey better than the destination. We suggest that you do your shopping by bike. So never leave the bikes behind again because you 'don't know where to ride' if you go on holiday to KwaZulu-Natal.

Mpumalanga

The landlocked Mpumalanga province is host to the largest commercial forest in the world. At the escarpment, mountainous terrain sheers off dramatically to the Lowveld and coastal plains of Mozambique in the blue distance.

The capital of off-road cycling is the little town of Sabie, where local riders have worked with forestry landowners to create a hub of delectable off-road rides carpeted with pine needles and infused with oxygen. If you decide to visit the Lowveld, do not miss an unforgettable wild ride with the big five in the Kruger National Park. An amazing experience at a price that local cyclists can definitely afford.

Free State

In 1990, the Koranna Two Mountains Trail was the first official off-road bicycle trail to be created and marketed in South Africa. Over a decade later, it has lost none of its allure for mountain bikers. These mountains thrust themselves up like lone sentinels in the flat countryside. The Koranna Mountains are also a fascinating window on South African history – stretching across the full spectrum from Bushmen to Koranna, Boer to Brit and now, of course, bicycles.

Limpopo Province

In an area that has been a migratory route since the dawn of mankind, Thabaphaswa was selected for its minute attention to detail in terms of creating a genuine ecotourism experience.

The Thabaphaswa Mountain, central to this ride, is a timeless landmark that travellers use to navigate their way going north (or south) on their travels into Africa.

BEST GRAVEL CRUISE

Province: Northern Cape **Closest Towns:** Upington/Augrabies **Distance:** 32–41km

...a ramble of gravel roads cavorts along the edge of the thundering Gariep Gorge...

AUGRABIES

Welcome to Planet Mountain Biking... Lunar ysterklip koppies shimmering through the midday mirage. Stark quiver tree silhouettes clawing high amongst a scurry of pointillist clouds. A persimmon sun dying into the dusk beyond the antediluvian bulk of Moon Rock, Africa's own Uluru. And through the amber chaos of this Augrabies stonescape, a ramble of gravel roads cavorts, scudding along the edge of the thundering Gariep Gorge, bisecting wide-sky plains and swooping playfully amongst contorted cacti and red-black rock. Along the downhill to Ararat, a family of giraffe arabesques across the road, stiff-legging away to where cumulonimbus clouds tumbleweed along the jagged horizon line. This is Aukoerebis, 'The Place of Great Noise', and you had better get ready for the joyride of your life!

Established as a national park in 1966 with the Augrabies Falls as its main attraction, this Northern Cape park rates as one of South Africa's flagship conservation areas. The impressive falls (the sixth largest in the world and with a volume exceeding that of the Victoria Falls) have carved a gargantuan 18km gorge through the granite-gneiss rock typical of the Bushmanland region.

The park, situated approximately 10km north of the small settlement of Augrabies, offers a variety of day hikes as well as the three-day Klipspringer Trail. Visitors can also go on night drives and do the unique Gariep 3-in-1 Adventure – a combination of canoeing down the gorge, hiking along an arid valley floor and then mountain biking back to the main camp. Although the riding is generally along well-maintained gravel roads, you might hit the occasional sandy or muddy patch depending on the time of year.

PREVIOUS PAGE: A heavenly sunset silhouettes a mountain biker looking out across the Augrabies Gorge.
LEFT: High speeds are possible along lazy curves meandering amidst ysterklip koppies and arid scrub.

30%

DISTANCE – A moderate 32–41km return ride

20%

TIME IN THE SADDLE – Around 2 hours

20%

DANGER – Corrugations in places, negligible on the whole

30%

TECHNICAL LEVEL – Excellent gravel roads, great surface

30%

GRADIENT – A few gentle hills, mostly level

20%

DIFFICULTY RATING – Easy

Rated by Jacques Marais

The setting

Day dawning upon the surreal Augrabies landscape may easily lead you to believe you have been beamed into a strange and distant corner of our solar system. Weird forms take shape and all manner of reptiles, insects, birds and mammals come to life.

Vibrantly coloured lizards and rock agamas scurry into action, malachite kingfishers preen alongside still rock pools and klipspringers flaunt their sure-footedness along gorge cliffs. Gemsbok, giraffe and endangered black rhino roam here upon the arid Nama Karoo scrubland, a biome within which minute vygies, kokerboom and stands of white karee flourish.

Strange tales are rife within this mythological land where dinosaur fossils have been frozen in rock since time immemorial and legend has it that a cattle-gobbling river snake guards the 130m-deep pool at the base of the falls.

Even though you may never have the pleasure of meeting this monster, the incredible fauna and flora show (and the gigantic river barbel) will more than make up for it.

How to get there

Follow the N14 (R64) west from Upington past Keimoes towards the small fruit-growing town of Kakamas (92km). Exactly 8km further along the highway, the R359 turns right towards Augrabies – follow this tarred route through the town of Augrabies (25km) until you reach the park gate after a further 10km. The northern section of the park may be accessed via a gravel road heading northwest on the Keimoes side of Kakamas. SAA Airlink also offers regular flights to Upington.

Best ride

The gravel roads cruising along the southern section of the park are without a doubt the ride of choice and this easy, relatively flat route makes for an exuberant mountain biking experience. All levels of riders can have fun here, so make it a family day out. It is especially comforting to know that all the buffalo (not to mention the black rhino) are happily grazing on the opposite side of the Gariep River.

Start off from Main Camp along this undulating dirt ride, taking care when pedalling across the low-water crossing just over a kilometre out of camp. (It is covered in a generous slather of slippery moss and I performed a spectacular fall here while mapping the Augrabies route.) A few gentle climbs rising between rocky outcrops will

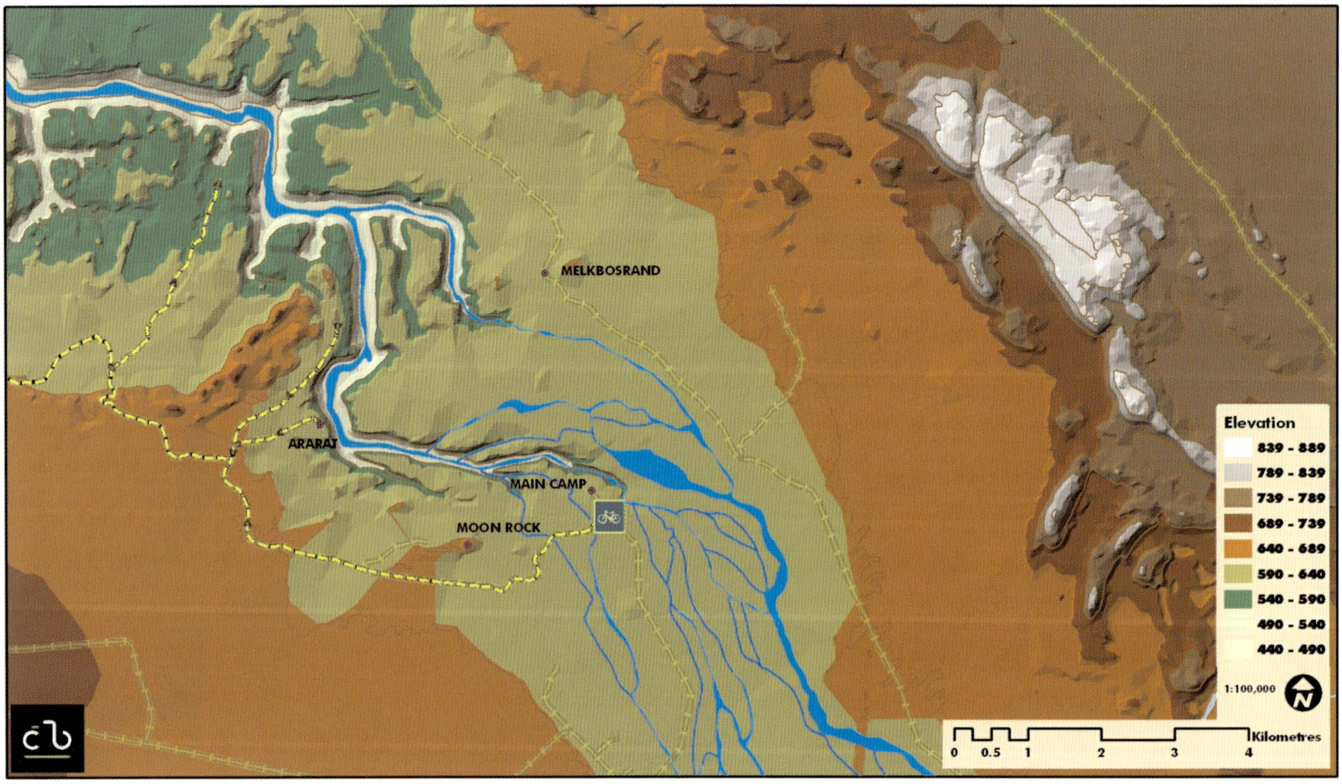

ABOVE: Beware moss-covered low-water crossings such as this one outside the main camp; cycle in as straight a line as possible to avoid slipping.

bring you to the turn-off to Moon Rock (5km) – turn right here for 1km to explore this magnificent magma mound.

Scan the dense camelthorn gullies for kudu and eland, pedalling back to the main road and on to where the track to the Ararat viewpoint branches off to the right (3km). Don't miss out on this: a slip-and-slide dirt chute brings you down onto the precipitous edge of the Augrabies Gorge, from where a wasteland view lurches up-river along the chaos of the rock canyon.

The return climb links you onto a dogleg right towards Oranjekom for a swashbuckling 2km free-ride and another spectacular panorama – don't rush, breathe, take in the view and revel in the hard rock splendour of this amazing place.

Once you're back on the main road, turn right and spin along for 2.3km – here the road forks left towards Fountain Lookout and right towards Echo Corner. Do the Fountain Lookout section (a 4.6km return) first, cruising the sandy flats to synch fully into desert mode. Then it's on to the *pièce de résistance* of your day out in Augrabies: the rollicking, ruckus of a run down into Echo Corner (3.8km from the main road). Here you may howl to your heart's content into the vastness of the surrounding plutonic rock or, even better, tune in to the immense sound of silence.

By now, the sun will be well into the big noon-day burn, so head straight back to main camp (14km), feeding on speed along the downhills and levels as you heed the call of the swimming pool. Mountain biking is a sadly neglected recreational activity in South Africa's national parks and Augrabies should therefore be complimented on promoting this easy and undulating off-road route. Gradient and road surface might not push your skills to the limit, but a fair turn of speed will up the excitement levels along the sloping home run. Keep your eyes on the road though – you never know when an elusive eland or gawky giraffe might amble across your way.

When to go

You're basically headed into semi-desert here, so expect those summer days to cook, especially between November and March. Plan your rides so that you leave camp at dawn and get back by around 11h00, then hit the swimming pool until the sun begins to dip down around 16h00.

Autumn to early spring makes for a gentler outdoor experience, although the nights and early mornings might freeze your butt off. Wear a shell and thermal gloves or cope with a severe case of MTB rigor mortis until the sun thaws your bones.

Other rides

Riemvasmaak, a conservation area encompassing 74 000 hectares of fascinating desert environment, was returned to the original Nama residents in 1994 during post-apartheid South Africa's first successful land restitution project. The so-called 'Riemvasmakers' settled around the original mission station and, with the assistance of the local tourism authorities and private partners, initiated a fledgling tourism project aimed at uplifting the community.

Mountain biking is just one of the outdoor action options on the adventure menu, with harsh rides happening on three 4x4 routes and along a dedicated MTB trail. Sand, rocks, stones, thorns, climbs, boulders – you will find them all in abundance along the edge of the spectacular granite canyon carved aeons ago by the Molopo River.

Maps for the **Perdepoort, Molopo** and **Deurspring** mountain bike routes are available from the information office at Riemvasmaak. Get there along a good (albeit sandy) dirt

HOW TO RIDE IN SAND

1) **Get tread** – fit wide tyres and deflate them to increase surface area even further. Make sure you keep them inflated enough to avoid snakebite.

2) **Ground control** – maintain a straight line and try to keep your front and rear wheels aligned while following the most compact line through the sand.

3) **Sit back** – move your weight as far back on the saddle as possible in order to wedge the rear wheel down and improve traction. This will also make steering easier.

4) **Spin city** – avoid jerky cranking by gearing down to a smaller ring and spinning evenly, thus maintaining consistent traction and avoiding rear wheel spin.

5) **Need for speed** – crank hard in order to build up a good head of steam before hitting the sand – this will help you maintain forward motion while you negotiate the area.

LEFT: Dizzying views and electrifying riding beckon at Aukoerebis, 'The Place of Great Noise'.
ABOVE: Easy riders bang into the looping bends curving down towards the Echo Corner viewpoint.

road snaking north from Kakamas to just west of the Augrabies National Park (a distance of 137km from Upington).

Another tempting option would be a day ride across the **Molopo salt pans** and up into the contorted rock world of the Lost City of the Kalahari. Saddle up for an early morning Zen session upon this surreal expanse to crank with dust devils across tracts of blistered mud and coarse salt fields. Beyond the shimmer of the pans, a craggy jeep track rises sharply to wind into a mesmerising world where soaring cliffs and tumbling escarpments mimic the shapes of a lost city straight from the pages of a Rider Haggard novel.

An endless network of gravel roads and jeep tracks winds amongst the rocky outcrops and windblown dunes for more

miles than you care to count, but be prepared for a ride that verges on the rough side. To get there, drive to Askham along the R360 before following the R31 in the direction of Koppieskraal Farm.

Off-the-bike entertainment

Tales of Northern Cape hospitality have attained legendary proportions and you may rest assured that the various accommodation and adventure establishments dotting the region around Augrabies into the red heart of the Kalahari and beyond will not disappoint. Dune tracking with Bushman guides at the Molopo Kalahari Lodge offers a fascinating insight into the fragile desert ecosystem, while a day of camel riding to the Lost City of the Kalahari from Koppieskraal Farm will leave you feeling like Lawrence of Arabia.

You are also only a few hours away from the magnificent Kgalagadi Transfrontier Park, an arid savannah expanse where oryx roam and huge black-maned lions survey their kingdom from vantage points atop amber dunes.

ABOVE AND OPPOSITE: The Gariep 3-in-1 Adventure offers gorge canoeing, desert hiking and off-road mountain biking. BELOW: The main route – one way. Various options can lengthen the route to 41km.

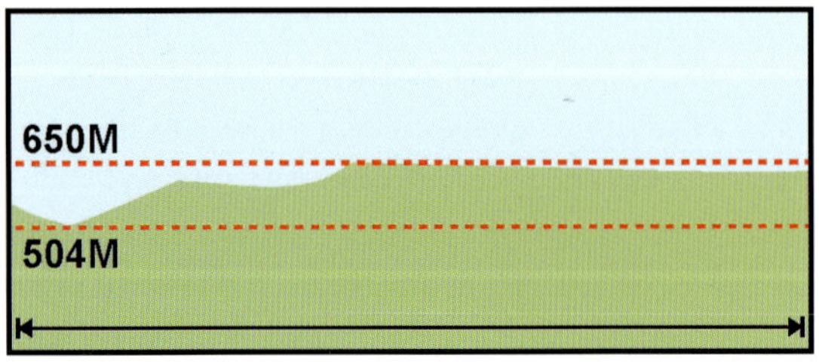

FAST FACTS

ROUTE
A return route with several optional add-on sections.

TRAFFIC
Game-viewing vehicles may stop without warning to check out cinnamon-breasted warblers.

ATTRACTIONS
Biking with giraffe; an awesome waterfall; canoeing along the Gariep Gorge; huge venison steaks.

START POINT
Augrabies Main Camp:
28°35.709' South, 20°20.321' East

FACILITIES
Fully serviced camp with chalets, shops, restaurant, swimming pools and Swedish tourists.

ENTRY FEE
Pay your park entry fee and you ride for free. Consider getting a Wild Card for major discounts.

CONTACT NUMBERS
Augrabies National Park: (054) 452-9200
www.parks-sa.co.za
Map info: Craig Beech at cbeech@mighty.co.za

BEWARE OF
Extreme temperatures, dehydration and snakes. Approach local wines with caution.

THUMBS DOWN
No night riding allowed. Perhaps in the future the National Parks authorities would arrange guided star-gazing rides?

BEST BACK COUNTRY BASH

Province: Eastern Cape **Closest Towns:** Bedford/Tarkastad **Distance:** 28.6km

Tumbling foothills surge abruptly along koppies and kranses before levelling out into gentler undulations along the higher slopes.

BAVIAANS

Let's get one thing straight. This is my backyard and I don't necessarily want a whole bunch of moegoes banging along a mountain I've known since my barefoot boerseun days. Fortunately though, this little piece of thornveld paradise is far enough off the major routes to keep most people away.

Those who do brave the dirt roads into the Baviaans River valley are sure to discover rollicking African trails traversing a landscape brimming with adventure, exhilaration and mind space beyond imagination. One person's hell is someone else's heaven, I suppose. So, if you don't appreciate gnashing gravel downhills, 10cm-long thorns, the full brunt of the sun and occasional encounters with pissed-off reptiles, this is a trail you should rather leave off your to-do list.

Despite its angular starkness and unpolished veneer, the countryside is undeniably beautiful and comes packaged with a rich African and colonial history. Faint Bushman paintings inside caves and overhangs time-line back to an era when the hunter-gatherers traversed these distant spurs of the Winterberg range. The arrival of the 1820 Settlers paved the way for the Baviaans River region to expand into prime agricultural country, although many current farmers have moved into commercial game farming since the 1990s.

Due in part to this latter shift in focus, a group of Bedford farmers decided to form the Baviaans River Conservancy. This environmental pooling of resources led to the establishment of a conservation area encompassing 76 000 hectares. Biking in the area is generally along good quality gravel roads, but a multitude of 4x4 trails and stock tracks offer technically challenging riding.

PREVIOUS PAGE: The route starts easily enough, following the river course, but later things get hectic.
LEFT: Traversing mountain grassland on top of the world near Buffelskloof Farm.

30%
DISTANCE – A moderate 28.6km circular ride

20%
TIME IN THE SADDLE – Around 2 hours

50%
DANGER – Rocky sections, devil and acacia thorns, cattle grids

50%
TECHNICAL LEVEL – Good gravel, eroded 4x4 tracks and paths

50%
GRADIENT – One steep hill plus a few moderate climbs

40%
DIFFICULTY RATING – Moderate

Rated by Jacques Marais

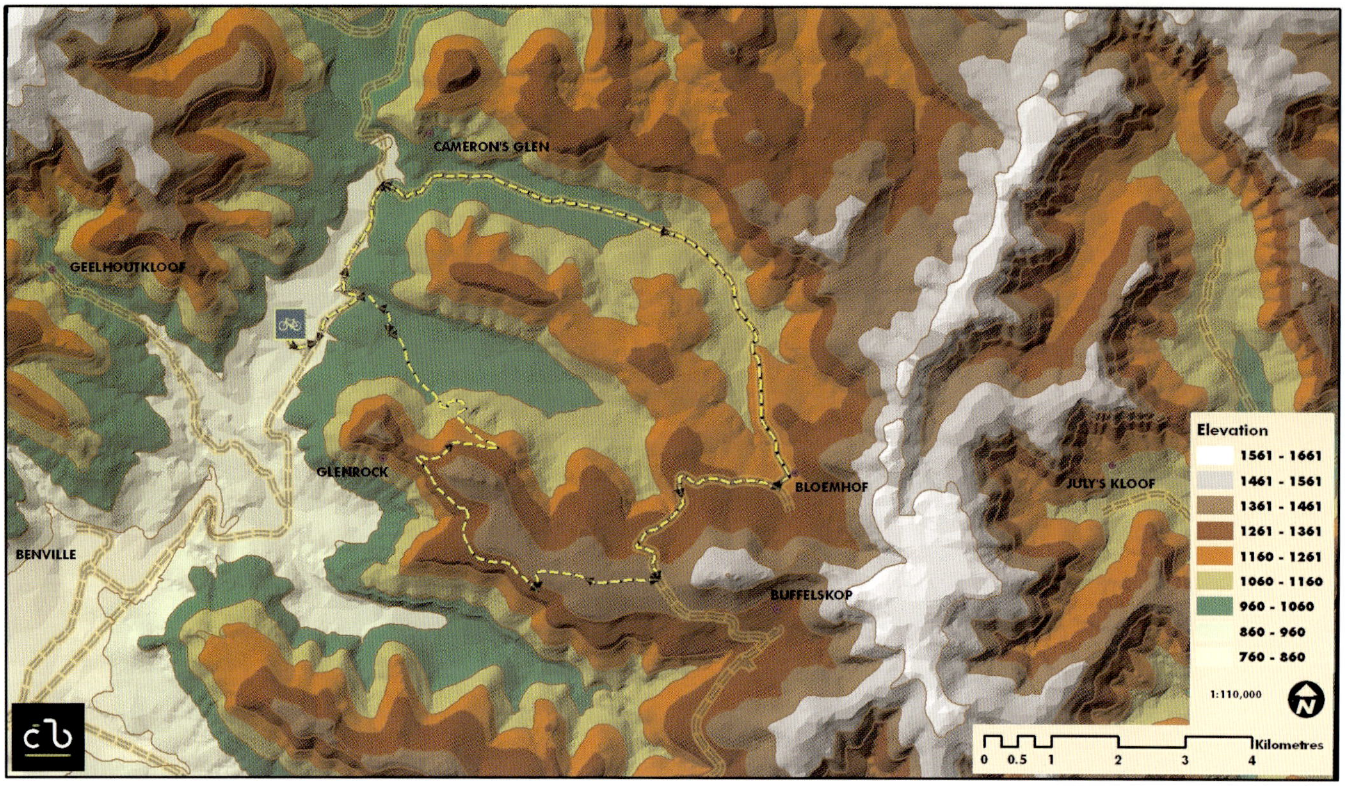

The setting

The Baviaans River Conservancy is characterised by a rugged (some would say hostile) topography rising up sharply from seasonal watercourses gouged into the arid Karroid plains. Tumbling foothills surge abruptly along characteristic ysterklip koppies and craggy sandstone or dolerite kranses before levelling out into the gentler undulations along the higher lying slopes.

Situated within the transitional zone between arid Karoo and temperate eastern grassland, the vegetation may generally be classified as false Karroid broken veld leading from valleys dense with acacias, semi-succulents and evergreen scrub onto grass-covered summits. This variation in habitat makes for a proportionally high bird count, with commonplace sightings of species such as brownhooded kingfisher, secretary bird and paradise flycatcher. Mammals are well represented, with kudu, grey rhebok, mountain reedbuck, fallow deer, aardwolf and caracal seen throughout the conservancy. Reptiles include mountain leguaan and more snakes than you could shake a stick at.

How to get there

Follow the N10 south from Cradock for approximately 80km before turning left onto the R63 at a sign indicating the route to Bedford and East London. Look out for a sign to Tarkastad via Baviaans River (10km before reaching Bedford) and turn left again, passing through a self-operated boom onto a secondary dirt road.

From here, you ascend along Wienand's Nek Pass before dropping down into the Baviaans River valley, a drive of 30km in total to your final destination of Silverbrook Farm.

Best ride

Twenty-three kudu. Herds of mountain reedbuck and grey rhebok. Baboon troops barking along a craggy skyline. A grumpy bushbuck ram barrelling from the underbrush. Assorted springbok, fallow deer, duiker and steenbuck. Black eagles, jackal buzzards and honey guides cruising the sky. Plus a 1.3m monitor lizard glaring from a rocky cleft in one of the dolerite cliffs. Just another perfect day of riding in the Baviaans River Conservancy...

Even without the phenomenal across-the-bar game viewing, this will still be an awesome ride. It starts off easy enough, cranking away from the Silverbrook homestead to cross the Baviaans River and join the gravel road between Bedford and Tarkastad (700m).

Cross the cattle grid and turn left along good hard-pack, banging over a narrow bridge before turning right through a gate signposted Buffelskloof (3.6km). Ascend gradually along what is essentially a farm road, passing the old Goedehoop homestead on your left (4.8km).

You will pass through several gates as you cycle along the valley floor past labourers' cottages and an old kraal (8.7km) before you reach Die Hoogte, your first steep hill of the day (10.6km). Click into your granny gear and climb onto the plateau for an easy cruise that will take you below the old Bloemhof farmstead. At 13km, another sign to Buffelskoof will direct you to your right just before you reach a stone kraal. Continue for 2.5km through four more gates, ignoring the road to your right 200m later to climb along a steep acacia ridge.

Look for a jeep track to your right at 16.5km (if you get to Buffelskloof gate, you've gone too far) and follow this dual track along a grassy plateau and through yet another gate (17.1km). Go along on top of the world for 2km and then start dropping down onto the opposite side of the spur along a helter-skelter dual track to an earth dam (20.1km). Trip along the edge of the escarpment with incredible views across the Baviaans River valley to your left, before again climbing slightly towards the Tor View gate (21.1km).

This is where it gets hectic. The next 2.4km will see you dropping nearly 300m along an eroded rock and gravel switchback liberally sprinkled with acacia thorns. Pass through the gate at the corrugated iron reservoir (24.2km) and blast along a speed section with a series of great jumps past a cement reservoir and a windmill at a gate (27.1km). Turn right here, pass through another gate after a few hundred metres and bear left where the tracks join until you T-bone with the Bedford road back near the first bridge that you crossed at the start of the ride.

Time to relax – turn left and cruise home back across the grid and to the Silverbrook homestead (28.6km).

BELOW: Rough riding as you drop down along a 4x4 track switchbacking towards Silverbrook Farm.

HOW TO STAY FRIENDS WITH THE FARMERS

1) **Gate crashing** – if you don't want to anger the locals, make sure you close gates once you've passed through. And make sure they're as secure as when you first got to them.

2) **Fence hopping** – if you get to a locked gate, you might be forced to jump the fence. Climb over at sturdy anchor posts where you're unlikely to do damage to the fence (or yourself).

3) **Dam dunking** – feel free to take a swim in the farm reservoirs, but don't toy with windmills, ball valves or outlets, as water is a life and death issue for animals on conservancy farms.

4) **Stock control** – don't blast into the centre of a herd of grazing sheep or cattle. Wild animals should be treated with even more respect, so ensure you don't get too close.

5) **Access area** – always get permission before cycling onto someone's land. If there are any traps or snare guns set for problem animals, you definitely need to know about this.

When to go

Want a weather report? 'Damn hot and dusty' should do it for around 300 days of the year, although thunderstorms have been known to strafe the ysterklip landscape during the summer months. Winter may be a completely different story though, with the big chill settling in for a few weeks between June and August. Snow, sleet and subzero temperatures will soon have you hauling out the Gore-Tex, so be prepared. Autumn and early spring go hand in hand with clear days and milder temperatures.

Other rides

There is, of course, also the other Baviaans. This is the renowned **Baviaanskloof Wilderness,** an area of more than 187 000 hectares stretching from Willowmore in the west to Hankey in the east. Hemmed in by the Kougakloof

OPPOSITE: An eagle's-eye view of the dry Baviaans River course with Tor View rising up in the distance.
ABOVE: Stop for a swim in the farm reservoirs; just don't toy with any of the gadgets!

and Baviaanskloof mountain ranges, this unspoiled 'Valley of the Baboons' is only accessible along the gnarly twist and swerve of the R332. The most obvious mountain biking challenge would be to take on this rough and ready, 170km gravel route. Start off from the Willowmore side if you want to benefit from the slight descent towards the coast, cycling away from the N9 and into the contorted ravine carved by the Baviaanskloof River.

The first major climb (after 37km) is along the gritty Nuwekloof Pass and you will ascend into a world of sandstone cliffs and tangled acacia trees along a road built by the famous Thomas Baine in the 1880s.

You can be sure of one thing while traversing the intense topography of these Cape Fold mountains: if you go down, you will definitely have to go up again. And vice versa. The gravel road scrabbles for a foothold along the steep slopes, reaching the nondescript little settlement of Studtis after a further 40km.

Yet another 25km of rugged isolation, with several river crossings along the way, follows before you reach Sandvlakte and the adjacent Coleske Farm.

It doesn't get any easier as you crank past remote farmsteads towards Smitskraal and the Kouga Dam, ascending into a seemingly endless mountain pass dipping and climbing amidst soaring amber kranses.

The road clings precariously to the steep and densely wooded slopes, carving a swathe through a profusion of indigenous vegetation spanning at least five divergent biomes. Giant yellowwood and stinkwood trees, assegai bush, ericas, proteas, geraniums, succulents, creepers and mosses flourish within micro-habitats ranging from montane woodland and valley bushveld to fynbos zones.

Animals and birds are abundant, with frequent sightings of kudu, klipspringer and other antelope, while there are still leopard reportedly roaming the higher ranges.

The attraction of the Baviaanskloof, South Africa's third largest wilderness area, is best experienced on a multi-day cycle. Overnight stops at self-catering farm cottages or camping sites such as Geelhoutsbos and Rooihoek are a must.

FAST FACTS

ROUTE
A circular route with steep hills and incredible views, starting and ending at Silverbrook Farm.

TRAFFIC
Farm bakkies, herds of angora goats or merino sheep and sleek, slow-moving cattle.

ATTRACTIONS
True bundu biking in an area teeming with game; experiencing African farm life.

START POINT
Silverbrook Farm:
32°27.532' South, 26°02.948' East

FACILITIES
Silverbrook is fully serviced, or go self-catering at the basic but beautiful Bloemhof House.

ENTRY FEE
If you stay on either of the farms, you ride for free. Day rides available at a nominal fee per bike.

CONTACT NUMBERS
Silverbrook farm: (046) 685-0712
bigidea@mweb.co.za
Map info: Craig Beech at cbeech@mighty.co.za

BEWARE OF
Chances are you'll come across snakes; acacia thorns scattered across wooded sections of trail.

THUMBS DOWN
The gates tend to break the natural rhythm of the ride. Because of all the thorns, make sure your wheels are puncture-proof.

Off-the-bike entertainment

Rural outdoor adventure is the order of the day in and around the Baviaans River Conservancy. This is no-holds-barred frontier country, and hunting, hill walking, horse riding and 4x4 trails feature big on the menu.

Anglo Boer War sites, affordable farm stays, authentic boerekos and offbeat characters (from butterfly collectors, artists and crafters to professional hunters) lend an unaffected charm to the area.

The Commando Drift Nature Reserve (Tarkastad) and the Mountain Zebra National Park (not too far from Cradock) offer additional birding and game-viewing opportunities beyond the borders of the conservancy. Then there is, of course, the historic town of Graaff-Reinet, the legendary Owl House at Nieu-Bethesda and the sublime beaches of the Sunshine Coast. All these attractions are situated within easy day drives from the Baviaans River Conservancy.

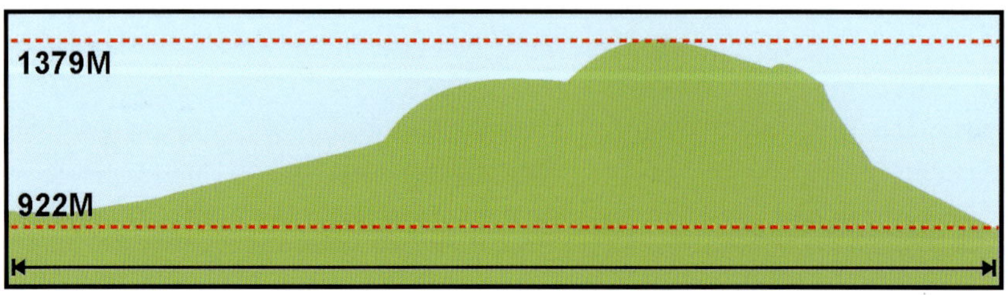

OPPOSITE: The deserted secondary road that links Bedford and Tarkastad offers miles and miles of easy riding.

BEST MULTI-DAY RIDE

Province: Western Cape **Closest Towns:** Citrusdal/Calvinia **Distance:** 172km

Bizarre rock sculptures rear sky-high above a lunar landscape to create an out-of-this-world mountain biking experience.

CEDERBERG

The Cederberg range, situated approximately two hours northeast of Cape Town, must rate as one of South Africa's most impressive mountain escapes. Here, bizarre rock sculptures rear sky-high in the mythical 'Valley of Red Gods' and the Maltese Cross towers above a lunar landscape to create a mountain biking experience that is out of this world. Rough-riding singletrack, never-ending gravel passes and fynbos jeep track – go and ride it now!

These days the term 'wilderness area' is often applied rather loosely to any small pocket of untouched nature situated beyond the ever-encroaching urban creep. The Cederberg, however, is a completely different story. Although the southern part of the range is situated so close to Cape Town, it harbours a vast pristine wilderness stretching from near Citrusdal in the south to beyond Clanwilliam in the north.

One of South Africa's premier hiking destinations, this sandstone paradise offers superb mountain biking, great fly-fishing, renowned rock climbing, challenging 4x4 drives and a unique outdoor experience within an extraordinary natural setting.

Most of the mountain biking will be along gravel roads and 4x4 tracks, so make very sure that you're tuned in to an endurance mood.

PREVIOUS PAGE: The mountains of the Dwarsrivier region and a lone rider are reflected in a tranquil farm dam. LEFT: Exhilarating riding awaits mountain bikers who venture onto the designated trails.

100%

DISTANCE – A 172km monster ride

100%

TIME IN THE SADDLE – 12–24 hours

50%

DANGER – High speed gravel downhills, rural traffic

60%

TECHNICAL LEVEL – Reasonable if you're on full-suspension

90%

GRADIENT – Several gruelling dirt road passes, a few flats along valley floors

80%

DIFFICULTY RATING – Difficult to extreme *Rated by Jacques Marais*

The setting

This is mountain fynbos country, but varied vegetation biomes (including Central Mountain Renosterveld, Succulent Karoo along the eastern extremes and Nama Karoo in the Clanwilliam area) grace the surreal sandstone landscape. Named for the rare and critically endangered *Widdringtonia cedarbergensis* or mountain cedar, the Cederberg forms part of the Cape Fold mountains, dating back a good 300 million years. Also known as 'The Rock Garden of the Gods', serene sandstone peaks, rugged ridges and fascinating shale formations encompass an area of 130 000 hectares dedicated to the preservation of numerous endemic plant species, including the rare snow protea. Animals, birds, reptiles, amphibians and insects are also well represented and, if you're lucky, you might catch a glimpse of anything from fairy flycatchers and klipspringers to elusive carnivores such as lynx and leopard.

How to get there

The N7 traces a picturesque route from Cape Town through the Swartland region, bypassing the towns of Malmesbury, Moorreesburg and Piketberg (154km) before rising sharply up Piekenierskloof Pass. From here, you descend into the scenic Olifants River Valley, with the Cederberg range skylining towards the east. Any number of gravel roads turning right will allow you access to the mountains, but the main route passes through Citrusdal and Clanwilliam, with the turn-off to the Algeria forest station 27km from Citrusdal.

Best rides

Tough call here, with countless riding options spiderwebbing along the valleys and slopes that grace the Cederberg Conservancy. Gravel roads and 4x4 tracks offer hundreds of kilometres of huff-and-puff along the Pakhuis, Uitkyk and other similarly steep passes, while dedicated singletrack MTB trails will bang you down right in the middle of this sandstone playground. Here are two favourite rides: one is longer, while the other is short and sweet. You decide.

Cederberg Roundabout

If you're up to a hardcore, multi-day ride, make friends with your saddle and pedal all the way around the mountain. Crank off from Algeria and into the teeth of the Uitkyk Pass before dropping down into the valley to follow the Driehoeks

OPPOSITE: Mountain bikers negotiate a section of singletrack near the Lot's Wife formation.

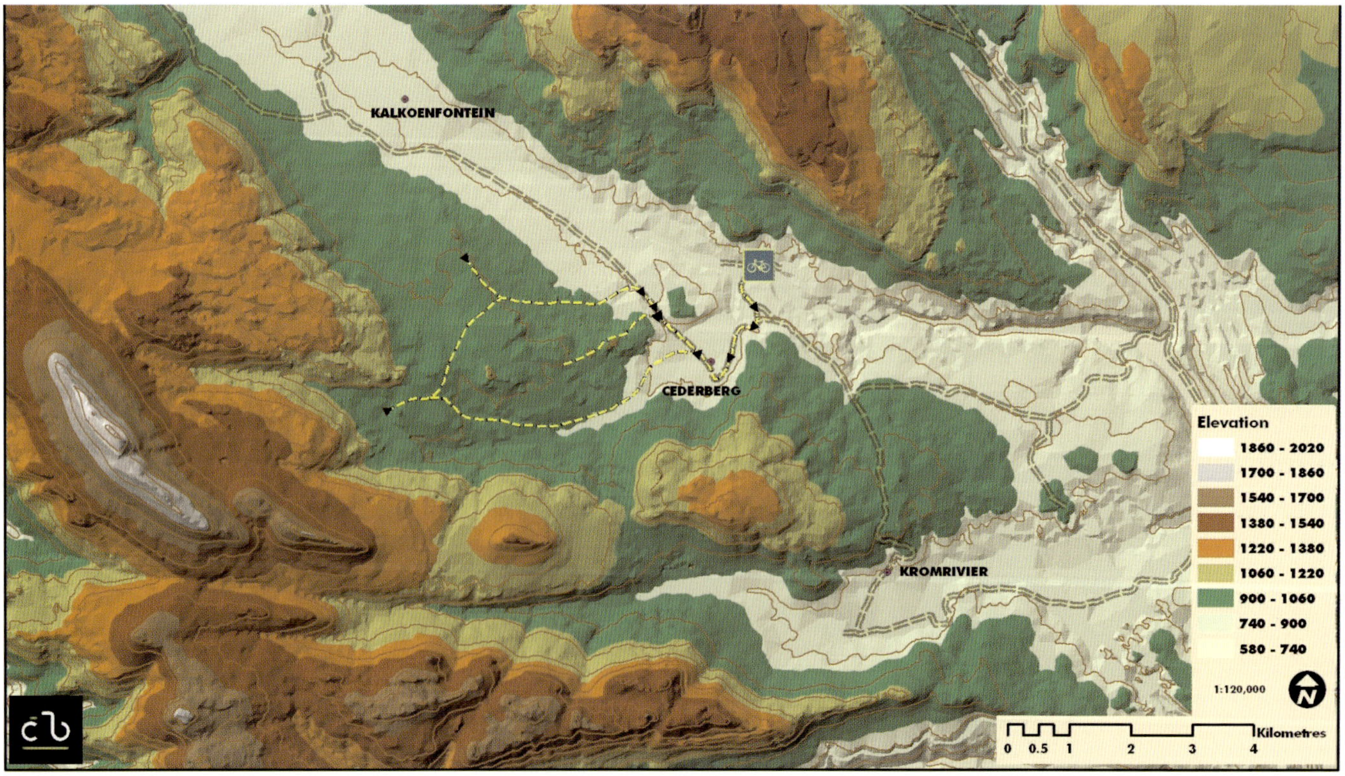

River past the scenic Dwarsrivier winery and towards Matjiesrivier (38km). Turn left here and get ready to bump and grind along the 4x4 route to the Moravian mission village of Wuppertal for a 35km trip into a little town that time forgot. If you have not worked in an overnight stop yet, this would be a good spot as you are looking at a gruelling 71km of gnarly gravel before reaching Clanwilliam.

Heads up for a short cut – turn left off the Heuningvlei road and do the push-and-carry boogie along a 5km section of hiking trail. (You save around 30km in distance, but you had better bargain on doing some heavy breathing along the way.) Enjoy the hospitality of this country town, then meander past the Clanwilliam Dam before granny-gearing up Rietvlei se Hoogte and on towards the cool and inviting river pools at Algeria camp site (28km). Accommodation options abound along the route, so plan your stages according to your personal level of fitness – remember, this is not a time trial; it is an adventure.

Lot's Wife MTB Route

This is one of those short and sweet sections of riding that make you believe in the gods of mountain biking. Start your ride from the Sanddrif camping grounds, crossing over the river and turning right towards Dwarsrivier (2km) as soon as you hit the Algeria gravel road. Climb for 1.2km past the vineyards on your right-hand side, continuing past the

LEFT: Technically adept riders will find ample options to hone their technique along the rocky ridges.

HOW TO SURVIVE AN ENDURO

1) **Plan ahead** – source route maps for the region, confirm land access arrangements and get a long-term weather forecast for the area.

2) **Maintenance, man** – make sure your bike has been properly serviced and that the frame set-up is spot-on for your body geometry. It's going to be a long, long ride.

3) **Emergency measures** – pack spare tubes, a tool kit, a cell phone (check reception along the route) and inform someone of your itinerary and estimated time of arrival.

4) **Body fuel** – replace the energy your body will burn on a long ride by constantly rehydrating (at least 1 litre every two hours) and eating (energy bars, trail snacks, fruit, nuts, etc.) regularly.

5) **Trust me on this one** – apply sunscreen constantly and, if you're cycling during the heat of the day, opt for loose-fitting, breathable clothing covering as much of your body as possible.

observatory turn-off until you see a sign indicating the Lot's Wife Hiking and MTB Trail to your left (a hand-drawn map is available at the Dwarsrivier Winery Office). Pump up the volume along a jamming stretch of singletrack, ducking and diving amongst cone bush protea and restios until the mountain bike route forks off to the right, dipping onto a jeep track dog-legging to the left past a pine tree plantation (3km).

Play in the shade for a while before tucking into the next 1.5km of singletracking. This will take you on a climb along a rocky incline before descending to T-bone with the Maltese Cross jeep track. Just on 2km of undulating hard-pack cycling past the Cederberg Observatory will link you back onto the Algeria road. Choices, choices – either head back to Sanddrif and that cooler box filled with ice cold frosties or hang left for another loop.

When to go

Winter riding in the Cederberg, although daunting for some, makes for a special experience. The sandy sections become more compact after rain, hectic summer temperatures drop to tolerable levels and you tend to have many of the trails and camping sites to yourself. And, if you are prepared to kit up for subzero temperatures, you might luck into the unforgettable experience of mountain biking through a fairytale Cederberg blanketed in snow.

Other rides

Another worthwhile MTB trail option is the 7.5km route starting from the **Sanddrif camp site**, climbing towards the Wolfberg Cracks parking lot (1km) before following a jeep track traversing left through the awe-inspiring Valley of the Red Gods. Crank amongst these towering sandstone pillars until you reach a stand of pine trees (2km), then bear left again onto a funky strip of singletrack. Go with the flow for a kilometre of freewheeling fun, then turn left onto the Rietgat jeep track to complete the circular ride back to the Sanddrif camp site.

If you fancy yourself as King or Queen of the Hill, **Kromrivier Farm** is around the corner – hit the hectic 4x4 trail to put your bike through a full-on suspension test.

Once you've done the Cederberg, explore mile upon mile of country road along the meandering **Middelberg Pass** dipping down into the Koue Bokkeveld.

Visit **Eselfontein Farm** to ride what must rate as one of South Africa's best-maintained singletrack routes. Deon Malherbe has transformed this superb route on his family farm near Ceres (which is also the venue for the annual Alexander Forbes MTB Challenge), into a mind-blast of a ride, that strings together a fast and furious 30km-plus of singletrack cycling. Speed sections are interspersed with thumping climbs and death-wish downhills, plus a sick mix of water crossings, wooden bridges and forest switchbacks. If we had space for an extra chapter in this book, then the Eselfontein route would be a dead ringer for it.

Off-the-bike entertainment

Kick back and relax at the Citrusdal Baths, experiencing the old-world Victorian charm while languishing in the liquid embrace of the 43°C outdoor and indoor mineral pools. Once you feel completely rejuvenated, explore the stunning kloofing routes, climbs and mountain hikes criss-crossing the Olifants River, Koue Bokkeveld, Nardouws, Pakhuis and Cederberg (there are more than 250 marked hiking routes in the Cederberg range alone).

If you prefer not to get high, hang low next to the tranquil Olifants River and cast a dry fly in an attempt to outwit a canny Clanwilliam yellowfish.

Slow down the day with an afternoon of wine tasting at Dwarsrivier Winery, an award-winning estate situated centrally within the Cederberg Conservancy.

Later, you can settle into an evening of star-studded entertainment at the Cederberg Observatory, less than 2km down the road from Dwarsrivier. Most Saturday evenings see amateur astronomers from Cape Town presenting lectures and slide shows at this venue.

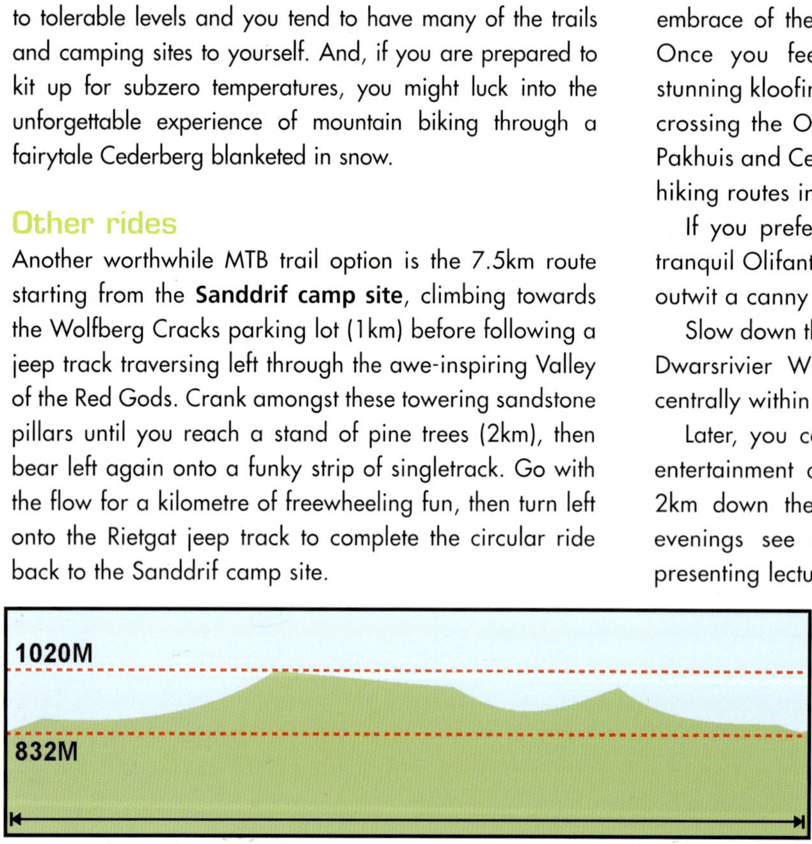

OPPOSITE: The valley floors, with their flat roads and towering sandstone pillars, offer a welcome respite from the gruelling dirt road passes.
LEFT: The map and profile feature the shorter Lot's Wife MTB route.

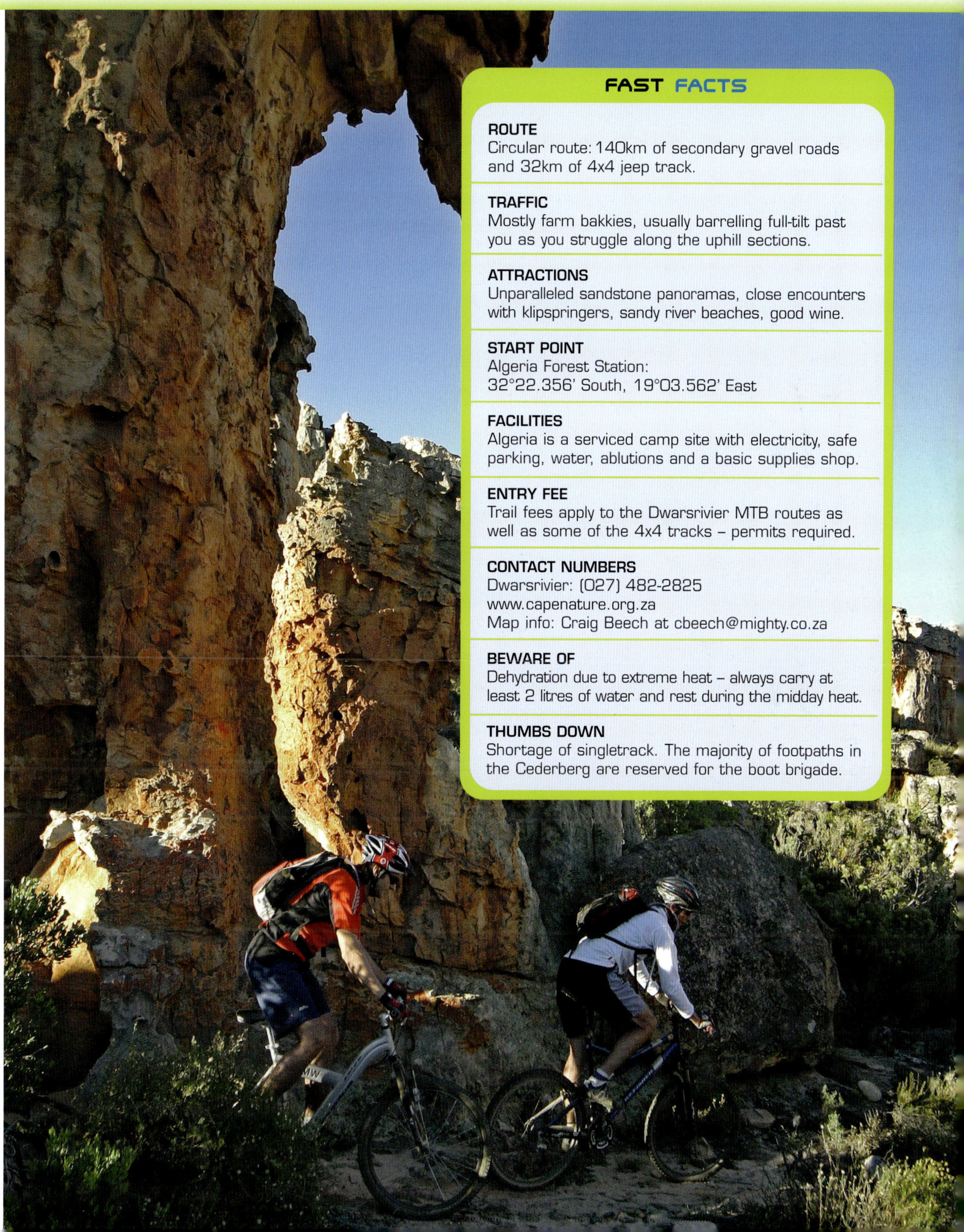

FAST FACTS

ROUTE
Circular route: 140km of secondary gravel roads and 32km of 4x4 jeep track.

TRAFFIC
Mostly farm bakkies, usually barrelling full-tilt past you as you struggle along the uphill sections.

ATTRACTIONS
Unparalleled sandstone panoramas, close encounters with klipspringers, sandy river beaches, good wine.

START POINT
Algeria Forest Station:
32°22.356' South, 19°03.562' East

FACILITIES
Algeria is a serviced camp site with electricity, safe parking, water, ablutions and a basic supplies shop.

ENTRY FEE
Trail fees apply to the Dwarsrivier MTB routes as well as some of the 4x4 tracks – permits required.

CONTACT NUMBERS
Dwarsrivier: (027) 482-2825
www.capenature.org.za
Map info: Craig Beech at cbeech@mighty.co.za

BEWARE OF
Dehydration due to extreme heat – always carry at least 2 litres of water and rest during the midday heat.

THUMBS DOWN
Shortage of singletrack. The majority of footpaths in the Cederberg are reserved for the boot brigade.

BEST METRO RIDE

Province: Gauteng Closest Town: Pretoria (Tshwane) Distance: 13.5km

Rocky terrain means challenging and very satisfying riding for the experienced mountain biker.

GROENKLOOF

Groenkloof Nature Reserve is a prime example of rehabilitation in progress in a nature conservation. A twenty-minute drive from the northern suburbs of Johannesburg and no more than five minutes from downtown Pretoria (Tshwane), the reserve is less frequented than the adjacent Fountains Valley. This latter resort has played a vital recreational and environmental role in the lives of Pretoria's citizens for more than a century (sophisticated Johannesburg to the south offers its citizens no such refuge). The scene of many picnics and braais, the resort can become exceptionally crowded during public holiday peak times and this certainly adds to the attraction of neighbouring Groenkloof.

The clear spring waters, plentiful game, fertile soil and scenic beauty of the valley have always drawn people here. Up until 1930, when the Vaal and Rietvlei dams were being built, all of Pretoria's water came from here. From 1915, shortages of wood and paper during the two world wars resulted in portions of the valley being leased to the Union government's Department of Agriculture and Forestry for commercial wood plantations. However, the environmental impact of thirsty alien plant species such as eucalyptus and pine was keenly felt in the late 1970s when the Apies River had been reduced to a mere trickle. An ambitious rehabilitation programme was launched to restore the valley to its natural state.

Thanks to the foresight of a few, a green gem of inestimable value is being redeemed, for the benefit of all.

PREVIOUS PAGE: For every climb there's a reward and you can gather some speed on the downhills.
LEFT: Riding neck to neck with the giraffes.

20%
DISTANCE – A short 13.5km

20%
TIME IN THE SADDLE – 2 hours

60%
DANGER – Fall potential on rocky singletrack

50%
TECHNICAL LEVEL – Rideable all the way for fit, skilled riders

50%
GRADIENT – Potential stalling and portage on rocky climbs

40%
DIFFICULTY RATING – Moderate

Rated by Herman Mills

The setting

High-rise buildings, urban sprawl, railways, major arterial roads and freeways hem in the Groenkloof Nature Reserve on every perimeter, so few folk outside Pretoria are even aware of this natural resource in the middle of the city. On any map, Groenkloof has a distinctive bell shape, with Christina de Wit Avenue and the Voortrekker Monument on the western and entrance side. To the east lies Fort Klapperkop and Nelson Mandela Drive.

Klapperkop Hill, which is a good example of an ongoing land rehabilitation programme, has recently become very conspicuous as it has systematically been denuded of alien vegetation. Throughout Groenkloof, you will also come across evidence of this programme in the form of felled trees, downed markers and obstructed paths.

The high dolomite content in the substrata is responsible for a fairly unstable geological composition that causes sinkholes. Rocky terrain means challenging and very satisfying riding for the experienced mountain biker.

Everything you see on this ride – from the geology to the flora and fauna – is slowly evolving back to its natural state.

How to get there

Take the Ben Schoeman Highway north and exit at the Eufees Road Interchange (M7 offramp). Turn right onto Eufees Road and go under the highway. You will see the main entrance to Fountains Valley directly in front of you. Groenkloof may be accessed indirectly via this gate, but it also has a direct entrance. Turn right onto Christina de Wit Avenue, travel 1km and the entrance is on the left, 800m from the Fountains Valley entrance.

Best ride

Commencing from underneath the towering pines at the start area, you initially ride out along a tarred road that used to service a drive-in during the 1960s. After a short, gradual climb the tar gives way to a rollicking jeep track through indigenous bush that takes you straight to the Nelson Mandela Drive fence line. Turn right and fly downhill with Klapperkop on your left shoulder and the Apies River flood plain to your right. Beware of flooding in this area as, during a good rainy season, the mud and water can cover your hubs in places – your feet will certainly get wet.

Once clear of the trees, turn left at the 4x4 playground and look for a rocky singletrack climb to the right. It is rideable all the way up, especially if you have a top-of-the-range, dual suspension bike and are not intimidated by the jolting of rocks.

HOW TO RIDE WATER CROSSINGS

1) **When you approach** a water crossing, your gear choice is crucial – both for negotiating the water and whatever is lurking underneath it, and for maintaining your momentum to exit up the other side.

2) **Keep your weight back** and off the front wheel as you go into the water so you don't go over the handlebars should you hit a hole or a slippery rock.

3) **Keep your focus** on where you want to go – if you look down into the water you can get disorientated and lose your balance.

4) **Spin through the bed** of the watercourse in an easy gear and try to maintain your forward momentum over whatever obstacles you may encounter.

5) **If it looks too rocky,** and the stream is fast flowing, it may be better just to get your feet wet, than to risk injuring yourself and spoiling the ride.

6) **If you know a ride** is going to have prolonged wet and muddy conditions, it is advisable to carry a bottle of chainlube. A wet chain is a dry chain and this adversely affects gear shifting. It also accelerates component wear.

At the top, pick your way through the felled gum plantation to the next fence line, turn right and follow this towards Christina de Wit Avenue.

Take your time: this is where you are most likely to view some of the resident Burchell's zebra superimposed against the city skyscapers, or you may be treated to seeing the 'two towers' – a unique skyline created by graceful giraffe and the landmark silhouette of the Telkom tower at UNISA. The indigenous game that has been reintroduced to the land is accustomed to humans and one can get very close. The track deteriorates as the gradient steepens, and there is a tricky

RIGHT: Take care in the rainy season as jeeptracks in the Apies River's flood plain can fill up with water and you might be up to your hubs in places.

corner at the bottom if you take it at speed. Take the next track up to the right, and then get comfortable with your granny gear as you take a steep jeep track climb to the left. Cross-country mountain goats will ride this one all the way up to the next turn. But those less prepared for an assault on gravity may choose the wrong gear or line or rider to follow and may well stall.

The next left turn is even steeper, but console yourself with the thought that the view at the top is more than worth the trouble of getting there.

You are now looking straight down onto Christina de Wit Avenue and should be able to see both the South African Air Force Monument and the Voortrekker Monument as you look at the city below you.

Being almost at the highest point in the reserve, you have some fun downhilling to look forward to, as well as a lovely little piece of technical singletrack that follows the contours of the hills on which you're riding.

Another viewpoint a little further along commands a panoramic view over the Pretoria CBD. You should see some antelope here too. Point your bike downhill and enjoy the last part of this ride.

The jeep track narrows to singletrack and, when you get to the road in the valley, turn left, practise jumping over the speed humps and follow the river valley all the way back down to the shady trees at the start.

Given the maze of evolving landmarks and trails you may get lost, but the reserve is not that extensive and is completely fenced in, so you need only follow the perimeter to find your way back to the parking area.

When to go

The moderate highveld climate makes it a pleasure all year round. In summer, the rainy season, beware of flooding.

It's also a good idea to plan your ride early in the morning – you may have difficulty in the extreme heat later.

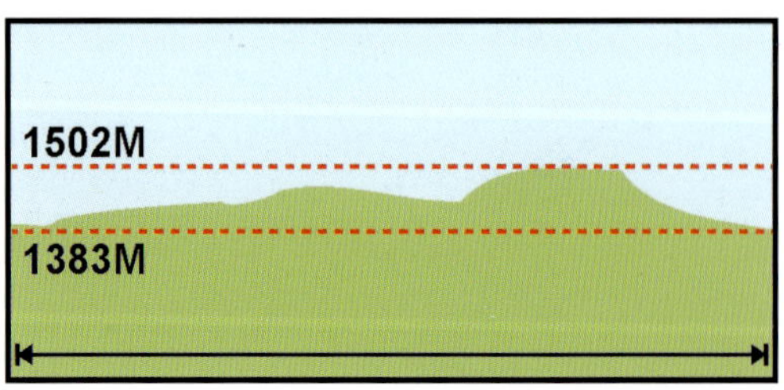

Other trail options

At the **Voortrekker Monument** there is a 7km circuit where you can cycle along the contours to relax, or go straight up and down if your aim is to train.

This is a very secure venue to cycle in with access control and security guards. The route is predominantly jeep track and takes cyclists through the nature reserve surrounding the monument. There is a nominal gate fee to pay per cyclist to enjoy this ride.

The **Fountains Valley Resort** offers a variety of twisty singletracks through the forests bordering the Fountains Park area. Challenging tracks and footpaths lead up Klapperkop Hill. Nature conservation authorities are fencing off these areas to address security issues.

At **Babbas Lodge**, 35km north of central Pretoria on the old Warmbaths road, you can choose your distance. It offers 10/20/40km marked routes in the Bultfontein area. Organised cross-country mountain bike races are held here throughout the year.

Off-the-bike entertainment

Many amenities are available along George Storrer Road. Mall rats will delight in Brooklyn Mall and Brooklyn Square that lie a mere 5km from Groenkloof and offer some 200 shops and restaurants.

If you just want to stop for a coffee or lunch, Cafe 41 Coffee Shop and Smoke Restaurant which are situated about 2km away from Groenkloof come highly recommended. There is also a Virgin Active gym and a public swimming pool within 3km of Fountains.

Drive through the 'Garden City' in November, when all the jacaranda trees lining the city streets are a riot of purple blooms. Also worth visiting in Pretoria are the Union Building gardens and the Art and Natural History museums.

Contact Tourism Information at (012) 337-4430 or visit www.tshwane.gov.za.

OPPOSITE: Everything you see on this ride – from the geology to the flora and fauna – is slowly returning to its natural state. Given the maze of evolving landmarks and trails, you may get lost, but the reserve is not that extensive and is completely fenced in. You need only follow the perimeter to find your way back to the parking area.

FAST FACTS

ROUTE
Circular route, with shorter or longer options. Technical singletrack and jeep track sections.

TRAFFIC
Shared with 4x4s and hikers.

ATTRACTIONS
A green lung from which to view the architectural and historic landmarks of Pretoria amongst non-predatory indigenous game.

START POINT
Picnic area:
25°78.873' South, 28°19.997' East

FACILITIES
Overnight hospitality offered in basic dormitory accommodation. Lapa, firewood and ablution facilities are available for overnight visitors. (Day visitors may use the picnic area.)

ENTRY FEE
Nominal entry fee. Monthly tickets available as well as discounts for scholars and children.

CONTACT NUMBERS
Groenkloof Nature Reserve: (012) 440-8316 or (012) 341-0591
davidb@tshwane.gov.za
Map info: Craig Beech at cbeech@mighty.co.za

BEWARE OF
Although many of the animals here are accustomed to humans, do not interfere with them.

THUMBS DOWN
The majority of the trail is shared with 4x4s – a dedicated mountain bike trail would be a great bonus.

ROCKIEST RIDE

Province: North West Closest Towns: Groot Marico/Zeerust/Koster Distance: 28km

...thick patches of bushveld cluster along watercourses, forming green veins between the bare-topped highveld hills...

GROOT MARICO

Groot Marico is a little riverside village in an unknown part of South Africa, so obscure that it was even overlooked by the Group Areas Act of 1950. As a consequence, it now has an Indian community that first settled here in the 1800s and was never moved away.

It is no coincidence that the trophies for the annual mountain bike race held here, the Groot Marico Mampoer Classic, are pieces of slate, since there is no shortage of this sedimentary rock that is the result of metamorphosis from quartzite. The tops of the hills are dolomitic, a geological feature that extends from Pretoria (Tshwane) right into the Kalahari Desert.

Water is what has given this area its life and its name. Marico is derived from the Setswana word 'Madikwe', the meaning of which has been obscured by the passage of time, but the images it conjures up are of blood, 'Madi' or crocodiles, 'Dikwena'. The 'Groot' of its name is to distinguish between the Groot Marico River and the Klein Marico River.

PREVIOUS PAGE: The timeless expanses of the Marico inspired Herman Charles Bosman, as they do today's mountain bikers.
LEFT: This typical slate-covered jeep track is a unique feature of the Marico district.

60%
DISTANCE – 28km, but technical riding makes up for any duration

40%
TIME IN THE SADDLE – 3–4 hours (Including walk and portage)

70%
DANGER – Rocks and loose slate

90%
TECHNICAL LEVEL – Extreme in places, unmerciful rocky terrain

80%
GRADIENT – Portages up and down

70%
DIFFICULTY RATING – Difficult. Ardent mountain bikers will die and go to off-road heaven

Rated by Herman Mills

The setting

With Groot Marico being in the transition zone between the highveld and the bushveld, there is a large variety of vegetation found here and various protea species can be seen flowering in midsummer. Dolomite, because of its unstable erosive nature, is the site of many springs of water as well as caves and sinkholes. There is a spring of crystal clear water called 'Die Oog van Marico', which is a natural swimming pool framed by water lilies with such clear water that one does not even need goggles to see underwater.

Situated 100km north in the Dwarsberg is Abajaterskop, once home to one of South Africa's literary greats: Herman Charles Bosman. Groot Marico is destined to become famous in the cycling world for its mile upon mile of unadulterated mountain biking pleasure. When you see the thick green bushveld clustered along watercourses like green veins running in between the swelling, bare-topped highveld hills, you know that you and your bicycle have come home.

How to get there

To reach Groot Marico, only two hours away from Johannesburg, start by driving west to Magaliesburg, following the Jameson route through Boons, Derby and Koster. From Koster to Lichtenburg, take the R52 for about 35km, turn right to Swartruggens on the R53. Travel for about 8km, then turn left to Zeerust on good gravel road. Travel past various turn-offs to the left and right. The gravel road turns into tar. After 1km on the tar, turn right to Kuilfontein. Drive a further 4km, then turn right to Groot Marico. Travel for less than 2km, and turn right to Draaifontein. The Stanton residence is on the left just after the drift.

From Pretoria (Tshwane) follow the N4 through Rustenburg to Swartruggens. Turn left onto the R53 at the stop in Swartruggens. Drive for about 25km, turn right to Zeerust onto a dirt road and follow directions as above.

Best ride

The ride discussed here is on Draaifontein, a farm that belongs to the Stanton family, and commences at either the guest cottage or the main homestead. You had better warm up first because the ride goes straight into an 800m-long climb with a gradient sometimes over 1:4. This long, technical and slate-covered climb will have you off the bike and

OPPOSITE: The Marico bushveld provides a vista that is ample encouragement to rest awhile and catch your breath.

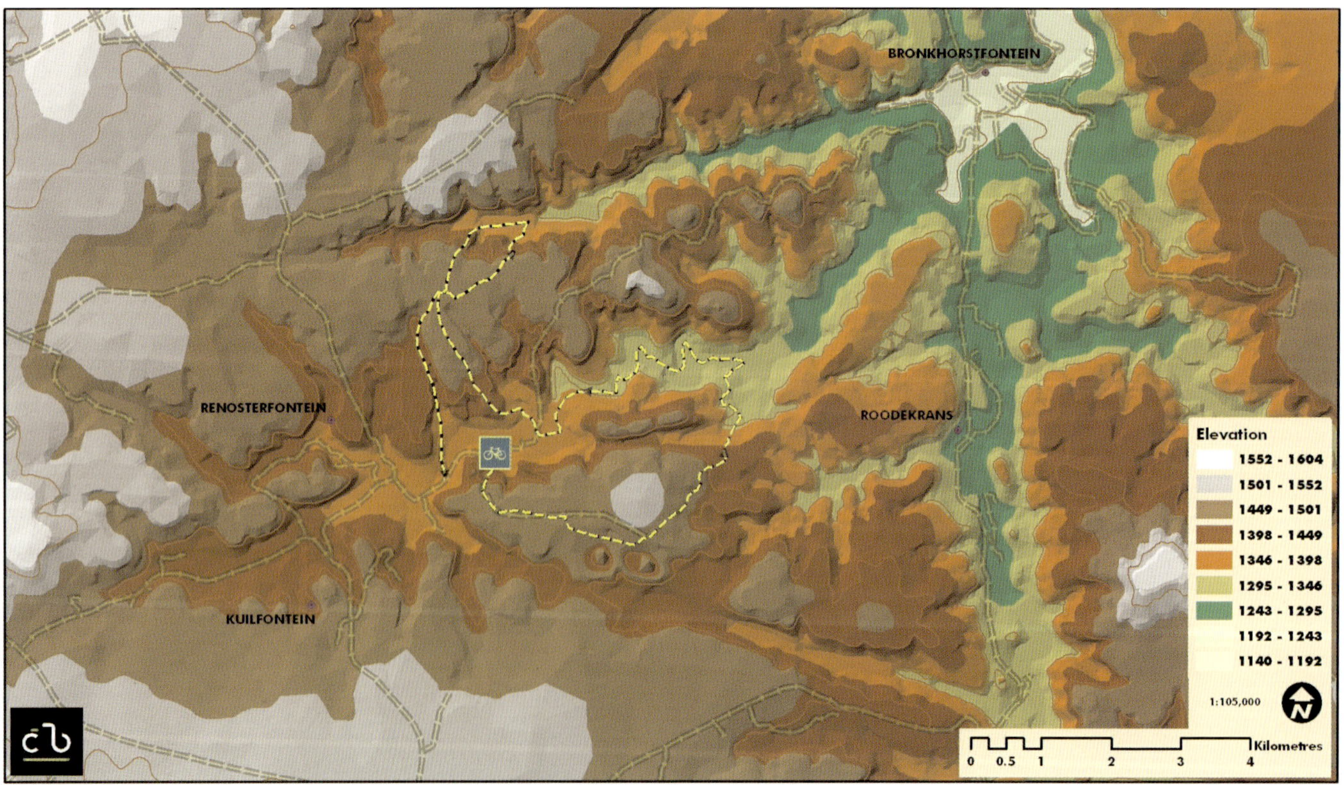

MET

HOW TO RIDE ROCKY HILLS

1) **Practice makes perfect** – recycle one of your old car tyres: being able to ride up and over it without putting your feet down will closely resemble how it feels to ride over rocks – especially the way that the hole in the middle of the tyre throws you and your bike off balance.

2) **Riding up a steep,** rocky slope is like doing interval training. Often your legs and lungs give in, long before your technical ability. To get to the top, you will need to be high intensity tolerant as well as superbly skilled.

3) **Take on bite-sized chunks** – choose your line intelligently, and commit to it. Usually on a rocky incline there is a little time to recover between very technical sections, allowing you to select your next line.

4) **Drop your elbows**, relax your upper body and keep your weight low over the bike and your front wheel on the climbs. Since you are going up, you need to keep your front wheel bedded into the terrain.

5) **Alternately sit and stand** according to what the rocks throw at you, in order to 'go with the flow' and keep control of your bike. Use your legs as additional suspension.

pushing unless you have that rare combination of high fitness and excellent bike handling skills. During the climb you will see typical bushveld vegetation, which changes abruptly to that of the highveld.

Here you will have to catch your breath in anticipation of the off-road treat to follow. Some nice fast, but tricky jeeptrack will take you around the back of a little hill and deposit you on the north-facing side. Pristine rolling hills and mountainous terrain all the way to the horizon present a perfect photo opportunity. The trail down to the valley below is really tricky. It's a veritable 'Satan's Alley' and only negotiable by riders with a predisposition to radical downhilling. Normal people will probably get hurt, so rather walk down so that you are left in one piece to finish the rest of the ride.

In the valley you will be swallowed up by riverine vegetation that provides welcome shade and coolness. After a prolonged water crossing, you are up the next hill negotiating loose slate and solid rocky banks again. A few little dips and drifts, and you veer off to the right straight down to the river below. Here you just follow the jeep track and blast through water crossing after water crossing, ten of them in total.

You ride in this bushy terrain for a while before the point where you can choose either to head home, or to tackle the second loop. If you decide to do the latter, you are in for yet another long, hot climb which will take you to a large farm gate. If you are too tired, you can go left and take the downhill home, or keep right and climb all the way to the top where some cement reservoirs are good for both a swim and filling up your water reserves. Carry on past the dams, and watch out for the road going down to the left. Speed monkeys can get their kicks on this downhill, where Isaac Newton does the pedalling for you. Once at the bottom, you should regroup before heading left past the drinking trough,

OPPOSITE: Only for the brave or those full of the famous Marico mampoer. Rather walk Satan's Alley than spend the rest of your ride in hell...
BELOW: Who cares about punctures when you can rest and enjoy scenery like this?

onto a cow path up the kloof. Here, some lovely singletrack created by the hooves and minds of cattle will keep you entertained until it gets too steep to ride. An 800m portage takes you back up to the top of the mountain and the farm dams. Go straight through the gate where you could have taken the shorter route earlier. A fast rolling downhill will take you down the mountain via a scenic gorge (again, with the odd water crossing thrown in) where you join with the main dirt road in a T-junction. Turn right here and listen carefully for those cold beers calling from your car just a few hundred yards down the road. If you are staying in the cottage, turn left for the delights offered by a soft bed. In summer this area becomes very hot, so it is advisable to ride early in the morning or late afternoon, with an adequate supply of water. In winter the nights are very cold, but you can get some genuine Groot Marico mampoer to keep you warm and cosy around the fire.

When to go

Autumn is beautiful and green after summer, with water in the rivers and pleasant temperatures. Summer gives cool nights and hot days, especially in the kloofs.

Temperatures vary between 15°C in the mornings, with max in the low 30s, but you do get very hot days where temperatures can rise to 40°C. In winter you'll find cold nights with frost, but warm days. Temperatures range from 0–25°C. Most of the region's rainfall takes place in summer and is interspersed by thunderstorms.

Other trail options

Lindbergh Lodge is a luxury game farm 40km from Wolmaransstad. Bikes are available for hire, or bring your own to ride the flat, easy self-guided rides on the plains, or stop to admire the weaver bird's version of cluster living in the acacia trees. (011) 884-8923

Annual mountain bike events include the Marico Mampoer Classic in April, 75/40/5km. (014) 537-3400

In June there is the Duiwelskop MTB Challenge, 58/30/10km near Brits, 082 324-6929, as well as the Magalies Monster, 70/35km, which takes place near Rustenburg. 084 513-3609

RIGHT: Good full-suspension bikes will not only help you maintain control on the seriously rocky stuff, but will add a level of comfort and confidence to increase your enjoyment of any trail.

Off-the-bike entertainment

There is Die Oog for scuba diving and swimming, 4x4 trails, mampoer shops, hiking trails and game viewing. For some genuine South African culture, there are two not-to-be-missed events. Between February and March of every year, Groot Marico hosts the Summer Sounds Festival, where jazz lovers can bask in mellow sounds. The third weekend of October every year sees the Herman Charles Bosman Literary Society celebrating the work of this famous writer in the form of plays, readings and poetry. His works are relived by some notable performers, one of them being the honorary life president of the Society, actor Patrick Mynhardt, who has specialised in performing Bosman for the last 30 years.

For more information visit www.marico.co.za or phone the Visitors' Information Centre on (014) 503-0085.

FAST FACTS

ROUTE
Approximately 28km of pure singletrack and jeep track. Very rocky in places, also sandy next to the river.

TRAFFIC
Cattle will be just about all you'll come across here.

ATTRACTIONS
Beautiful gorges and thick vegetation with abundant water crossings. Add to that a few really steep rocky singletracks to test your skills to the limit...

START POINT
Guesthouse at Draaifontein:
25°24.483' South, 29°2.316' East

FACILITIES
A comfortable guest cottage for 10 can be booked at Draaifontein for the weekend, or you can seriously rough it under a fabulous starry sky if you have the equipment to get you to their remote camp site: a 4x4 or raised bakkie required.

ENTRY FEE
There is a trail fee payable for day visitors. Those staying at Draaifontein ride for free.

CONTACT NUMBERS
Xonia Stanton: 014252 ask for 1812 (after hours). This is a party line with about 10 people plugged into it, so be patient.
Alternatively, contact Chris de Bruyn:
082 823-3815
Map info: Craig Beech at cbeech@mighty.co.za

BEWARE OF
Very rocky jeep track with loose slate.

THUMBS DOWN
Those riders who do not have good bike handling skills will find many parts of the ride rather stressful due to the technical nature of riding.

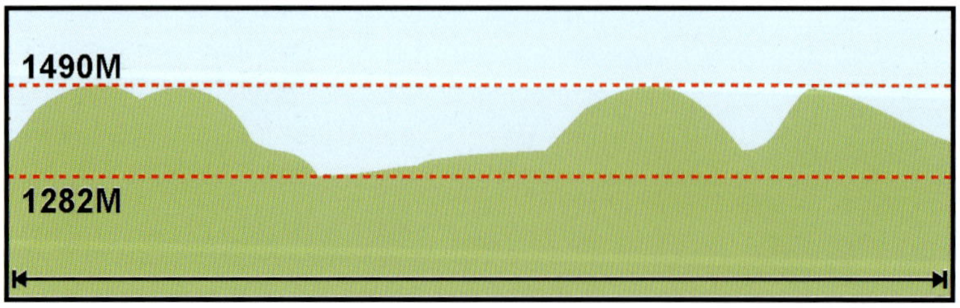

LEFT: On this ride, some cement reservoirs are good for both a swim and filling up your water reserves.
OPPOSITE: Numerous water crossings provide fun, entertainment and some welcome relief in summer.

BEST FANTASTICAL RIDE

Province: Eastern Cape **Closest Town:** Hogsback **Distance:** 23km

Hazy pine plantations, serene stands of indigenous woodland, high montane forest and sweeping slopes of grassland...

HOGSBACK

Sorry to do this to you guys, but there is a rumour that we need to quash right at the beginning of this chapter. Tolkien was NOT born in Hogsback, but spent the first years of his life in Bloemfontein. Don't allow that to detract from your visit to Hogsback, as the village and its leafy surroundings are sure to evoke the fantasy landscapes of the Shire and beyond. If you have read *Lord of The Rings* or seen the blockbuster movies, the fantasy forests encircling this sleepy little village will transport you into the epicentre of a modern-day Middle Earth. Hazy pine plantations, serene stands of indigenous woodland, high montane forest and sweeping slopes of grassland compose a jade mosaic unfolding in the shadow of razorback rock ridges.

Situated in the mountainous Amatole region of the Eastern Cape, the village is set centrally within a logging area operated by the Department of Water Affairs and Forestry and is named after the three ridged summits (reminiscent of the bristly backed wild pigs found in the area) that form part of the Amatole range. Hogsback itself is perched upon the western rim of the inland escarpment and overlooks the rural valley of Tyume, a fertile dale dotted with Xhosa huts and grazing cattle. The forests, plantations, valleys and slopes of the region are overrun with forestry roads, cattle tracks, 4x4 routes and singletracks, offering mountain biking along a diverse mix of terrain. Keep in mind that the mountainous nature of the area equates to more than just the occasional climb, while the high rainfall makes mud a certainty.

PREVIOUS PAGE: Wooden signs guide you along many sections of the trail.
LEFT: High ridges with rocky razorback spurs led to early settlers naming the village 'Hogsback'.

20%

DISTANCE – A shortish 23km circular ride

30%

TIME IN THE SADDLE – 2–3 hours

60%

DANGER – Ramps, fallen trees, brambles, slippery surfaces

50%

TECHNICAL LEVEL – Varies from reasonable gravel surfaces, deep mud and overgrown tracks to loose rocks

50%

GRADIENT – You'll spend 60–70% of your time climbing; one especially steep 2km climb

40%

RATING – Moderate to difficult

Rated by Jacques Marais

The setting

Nestling within the peaceful heart of the Amatole Mountains approximately halfway between Adelaide and Stutterheim, the remote mountain retreat of Hogsback epitomises nature at its tranquil best. An altitude of nearly 1 400m above sea level has blessed the village with cool summers and a high rainfall, thus contributing to the extraordinarily lush forests, abundant water and profusion of wild berries. Nature lovers, artists, crafters, hikers, mountain bikers and anglers all come here to seek regeneration at the shrine of the great outdoors – revitalising mind, body and soul in ethereal surroundings resplendent with the rush of waterfalls and cascading forest streams. Ancient trees, some estimated to be more than 800 years old, grace lush glades thick with yellowwood, white stinkwood, knobwood, white ironwood, sneezewood and Cape chestnut. Dainty harebells, fields of arum lilies and splashes of agapanthus colour the fecund undergrowth amongst the roil of blackberries and brambles. Soak up the silence of quiet glades where, if you wait long enough, you might be rewarded with the feathery flash of a Knysna lourie or Cape parrot while listening to the chattering of samango monkeys echoing in the canopy overhead.

How to get there

Follow the N2 east in the direction of King William's Town and then turn left onto the R63 once you reach this quaint Settlers town. After approximately 65km, bear north along the R345 for around 40km along a reasonable tarmac road leading straight to Hogsback (note that the surface deteriorates as you approach town and the final 3km is along rough gravel with the occasional pothole, so take it easy).

Best ride

Security in and around Hogsback is often a bit of a talking point, but I can categorically state that I did not sense even the slightest aggression or danger on my visit to the area. It is, however, a region characterised by the vast divide prevalent between the haves and have-nots of our beautiful country, so rather be safe than sorry.

Cycle in a group if you feel uncertain, speak to the locals regarding the safest route and leave an itinerary with someone who will check up on your return. Your best option

OPPOSITE: A GPS is an excellent tool when you are navigating forest trails and will assist you in finding your way, even in the most challenging of situations.

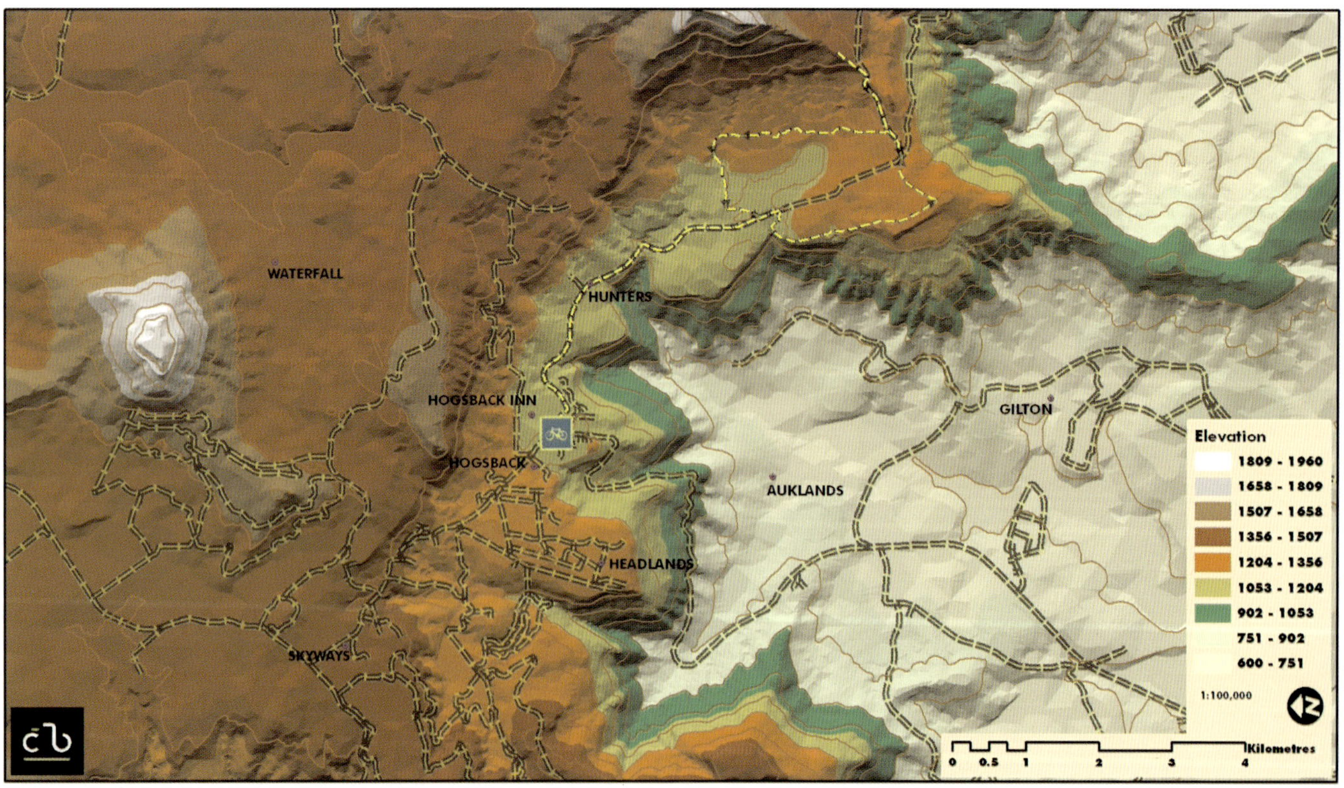

HOW NOT TO GET LOST IN THE FOREST

1) **Have map, will ride** – if your route is not marked, try to get a map of the area. A detailed topographical map is best, but even a basic map hand-drawn by a local might help in a worst case scenario.

2) **Be alert while you ride** – constantly observing the topography and natural features along the way. This will help you position yourself within the surrounding landscape.

3) **Back-track boogie** – if in doubt, opt to retrace your route by following your bicycle tracks in a reverse direction until the landscape once again makes a bit of sense.

4) **Get direction –** use the sun, moon, stars and nature to help you determine direction. In the southern hemisphere, moss grows on the southern side of trees or rocks, while flowers bend towards the north.

5) **Tech junkie** – a GPS loaded with local electronic maps and fitted to your handlebars makes getting lost impossible. Just make sure you take a set of spare batteries.

FAST FACTS

ROUTE
Circular or return route along gravel road, jeep track and singletrack with possible permutations.

TRAFFIC
Occasional taxis and heavily laden bakkies trawl the gravel strip towards Zingcuka and Keiskammahoek.

ATTRACTIONS
Ancient trees, tranquil forest lakes, trout streams, waterfalls, rich bird life, heaps of old world charm.

START POINT
Trailhead:
32°35.749' South, 26°56.238' East

FACILITIES
Hogsback Inn: (045) 962-1006 or
www.hogsbackinn.co.za
Hogsback Backpackers Lodge (they hire out mountain bikes): (045) 962-1031

ENTRY FEE
Permit required – can be obtained from hotel reception. Free riding along all public gravel roads.

CONTACT NUMBERS
Hogsback Tourism Office: (045) 962-1130
incite@lantic.net
Eastern Cape Tourism: (043) 701-9600
www.ectourism.co.za
Map info: Craig Beech at cbeech@mighty.co.za

BEWARE OF
Breaking your neck along ramps slippery with moss and frost, thick fog, dead trees across track.

THUMBS DOWN
Sadly, neglect and a lack of maintenance have turned 70% of the official trail into a bundu-bash affair.

is to use the safe parking at ye olde Hogsback Inn and kick off your ride at the gate leading from their rambling country garden. From here, Wolfridge Road blasts dead centre into the tree-filled playground that unfolds from the village towards the three Hogsback ridges. Now for some good news: to the left of the gentle gravel descent, you will find an adrenalin-inducing singletrack route replete with wooden ramps, drop-offs and boardwalk bridges created specifically for mountain bikers. Sadly, at the time of writing, this route was in serious need of maintenance, with brambles and branches clogging large sections of what otherwise would surely be the ride of your life. Do not be discouraged though, as there are some sections still open for play, although you might have to detour along the gravel road every so often as you descend towards the Tyume River (3.5km).

To your right, there is a short hiking trail down to the Madonna and Child waterfall – this is an excursion not to be missed, but I would advise that you carry your bike down with you or leave someone to look after the bikes. From here, you have two options: either stick to the road to Zingcuka for a hectic 2km climb or turn right along a track following the escarpment around to first Robinson Falls and then Robinson Dam (5km) back on the main gravel road. Immediately after the dam, turn right again towards the viewpoint across the Tyume valley, cycling along a shady two-spoor track past a small dam (6.3km) before climbing steeply to the 1 222m trig beacon (7.7km).

A gravel chute swoops from here back down to the Zingcuka road (8.5km), where you dog-leg first right and then left along the access road to the 4x4 track ascending steeply towards the serrated edge of the high Hogsback ridge. I explored further up the mountain road for a few kilometres, but back-tracked to turn left at 9.2km, following an overgrown track contouring along the slope parallel to the main road. After 2km of stump jumping and dead tree dodging, you can try to follow the Deodar loop indicated on the Hogsback MTB map, but might have to retreat to the Double T-junction and zigzag down to Robinson Dam to rejoin the Zingcuka road (12.9km). From here, you could opt for a straight run back to Hogsback Inn along the main road (6.3km) or turn right 400m after crossing the Tyume to follow the Holy Cypress trail past Hobbiton through stands of sequoia and indigenous yellowwoods before joining Oak Avenue to return to the village (8.7km).

When to go

Got to go with the old cliché here, because Hogsback truly is a bike town for all seasons. Breezy, berry-picking summer days, the crisp spring and autumn weather as well as wet, English winters (with periodic snowfalls) all come with their own attractions. Frequent thunderstorms occur between October and February. The results are usually instant 'pea soup' fog and bogs that come hand in hand with an annual rainfall of 1 270mm.

Other rides

Please note that the route described under Best ride was my personal selection and that any number of other permutations are possible in the area. The three rides on the original MTB route map all set off along the verge of Wolfridge Road up to where the Holy Cypress section forks left just before the Tyume River to loop back into the village in an anti-clockwise direction. A section of the Deodar Loop can be done by branching off right from the Holy Cypress or continuing past the Double T-junction, but be prepared for a major bundu-bash. My ride very much followed a combination of the Zingcuka road and the Madonna Loop, but in an anti-clockwise direction. This option is eminently rideable, but it will be well worth your while to speak to the locals to get an on-the-ground update before you set off. Who knows, maybe the local municipality might even clear that amazing section of singletrack that is going to waste as we speak.

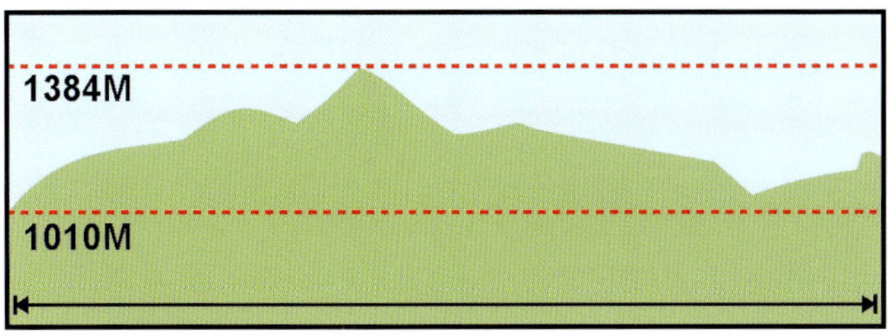

Off-the-bike entertainment

For those who do manage to pry their butts out of the saddle, an outdoor playground of note awaits exploration. Superb day walks and hikes (including the 100km, linear Amatola Trail), a selection of horse and 4x4 trails, peak- and rock-climbing routes, fly-fishing, the famous Sandile caves, rock art sites, bird watching and tree spotting are but a few of the outdoor options.

Hogsback is also a haven for artists and crafters, with numerous galleries and shops offering anything from woodcraft and pottery to sculptures and paintings.

The Vukani Buddhist Meditation Retreat, Frontier War sites, the anti-apartheid museum at Fort Hare and the Spring Music Festival also all draw numerous visitors to this beautiful area of the Cape.

Below: The Hogsback trail traverses steep slopes blanketed in dense indigenous forest with views across rural valleys.

BEST JUST-OUT-OF-TOWN RIDE

Province: Gauteng Closest Towns: Magaliesburg village/Rustenburg Distance: 24km

Gentle grass plains give way to steeper slopes scattered with rocks and boulders...

INGWE

Ingwe Bush Camp has great historical credentials, but best of all, Gary Fisher, that founding father of off-road cycling, once rode here. This property is a working farm that has been in the Saunders family since those pioneering days of the 1800s. The original homestead, established in 1867, is still occupied today. Both game and cattle form the core business, but twenty years ago the family had the foresight to develop their property for conservation. Consequently, one of only three vulture restaurants in the Magaliesberg is situated here, this one on top of an imposing section of the Magaliesberg massif. Little wonder, for this is the highest point in the range, and the peak is called Nooitgedacht.

This feature did not go unnoticed during the Boer War, when British forces under General Clements set up a signalling station here. On 13 December 1900, the Boers, under General de la Rey, used speed, surprise and their knowledge of the terrain against their enemies. British forces both on top of the mountain and in the kloof were put to rout by the Boers, with the most savage fighting taking place right on the edge of the kloof precipice. In what became known as the Battle of Nooitgedacht, the doomed British heliograph operator just managed to signal defeat before plummeting to his death on the rocks below.

Today, your only battle would be the terrain that you're about to encounter.

PREVIOUS PAGE: Fitter, more experienced riders will be unable to resist the lure of altitude. A rude awakening lurks on the first steep, rocky climb up the scree slopes, but thereafter, the jeep track rolls up and down. LEFT: Ingwe offers both typical African grasslands and mountainous terrain in one neat package.

40%
DISTANCE – A short 24km

20%
TIME IN THE SADDLE – 2–3 hours

20%
DANGER – Short sections of jeep track may be eroded. Scary fast downhill on concrete

50%
TECHNICAL LEVEL – Only one short, steep technical climb

60%
GRADIENT – One very steep, paved climb up the kloof

40%
DIFFICULTY RATING – Moderate

Rated by Herman Mills

The setting

It is virtually impossible to get lost while cycling here since the farm is set against the southern slopes of the Magaliesberg mountains. Gentle grass plains give way to steeper slopes scattered with rocks and boulders that have eroded off the ancient sandstone cliffs thrusting up into the sky. At an estimated 400 million years, they are the second oldest rock formation in the world. On a clear day, these imposing cliffs are visible from the northwestern suburbs of Johannesburg, 70km away.

Ingwe has an abundance of non-predatory wild animals. With 25 species in all, amongst them giraffe, kudu, eland, zebra and nyala, the viewing of African game at the tips of your bar-ends is guaranteed. The only exception is the namesake of the property, the solitary and self-sufficient leopard, which is rapidly having to adapt to living in close proximity to major urban settlements.

Another star attraction is the vultures. These magnificent birds of carrion, with wingspans of almost two metres, faced an uncertain future twenty years ago due to the destruction of their habitat, but conservation efforts have led to the Magaliesberg being host to one of three breeding colonies. The vulture restaurant at Ingwe feeds over 400 birds. Sightings of Cape griffin, lappet-faced vultures and white-backed vultures are guaranteed.

How to get there

Take the R563 from Krugersdorp. 3km after the Hekpoort Pass, turn left onto the R560 from Hartbeespoort. Travel 2km and then turn right onto a dirt road at the 'Bird Store', the general dealer. After travelling 7km look for the Ingwe entrance to your right. The venue is well signposted.

Best ride

Embarking from the tented camp and conference centre under a verdant canopy of indigenous trees, the track leaves the cool, moist forest too soon and goes on grass-lined hard-pack jeep track parallel to the mountain range. Travelling in a westerly direction across the plains, some of the resident herds of antelope can be seen at a distance.

Novice riders may wish to hug the contours in this area, since the only other option is going straight up and then doubling back east. Fitter, more experienced riders will be unable to resist the lure of altitude. A rude awakening lurks

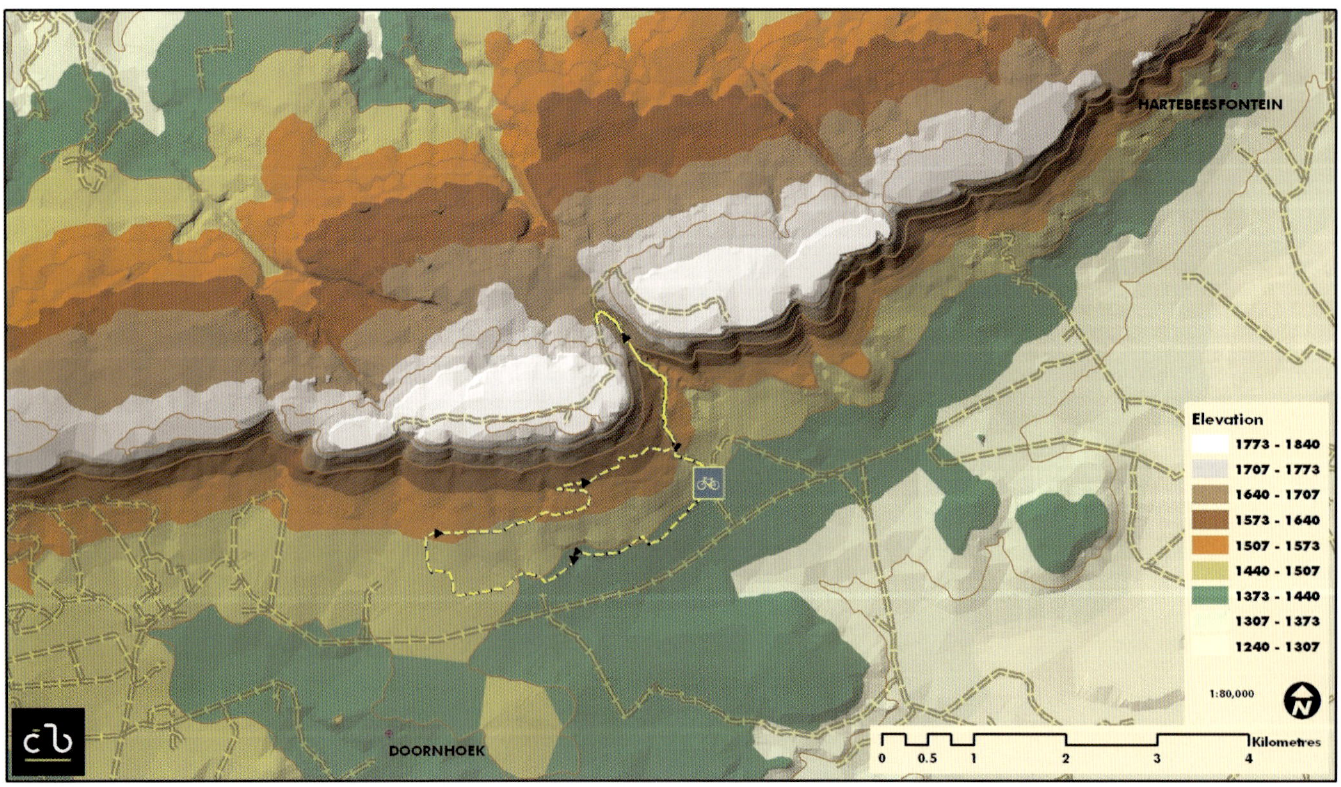

on the first steep, rocky climb up the scree slopes, for all but the fittest and most technically dextrous riders will be off their bikes and pushing. Thereafter, the jeep track literally rocks: testing your nerves and skills. The track rolls up, down and around the folds at the foot of the impressive cliffs you are fast approaching. After good rains there are plenty of large puddles thrown into the trail mix as well. This is such focused riding that it is difficult to remember there's more to look at than the rough terrain up ahead that will soon pass under your wheels. But joining the concrete road up Nooitgedacht Kloof is a reality check of note.

Look down – you will see the Ingwe entrance gate far below and the orderly farms of Hekpoort fading into the distance. Look up, and you will see an irresistible climb into the mysterious kloof.

None but the fittest riders will be able to pedal all the way up, but pushing the bike gives one time to listen to the stream trickling down the kloof. Time to reflect uneasily on the battle that was fought at the edge of those ominous steep cliffs monopolising the sky. Just before it becomes too quiet, a distinct change in flora announces that you have almost reached the mountain top.

Concrete gives way to dirt again and you can see the microwave relay towers that are at 6 068ft above sea level. It is now possible to view all of 'Die Moot' from Hartbeespoort Dam to Pretoria (Tshwane) in the east. It would also be around about now that you may get a whiff of vulture 'haute cuisine à la carrion'.

The saddest thing about mountain biking is that an incline that may take two hours of climbing flashes past in a mere ten minutes of rim-melting descent. All roads on the right when you go down the concrete take you back to camp. Enjoy this lovely ride and remember to take the time to savour your surroundings.

BELOW: The modern microwave relay station marks the site of the Battle of Nooitgedacht during the Anglo-Boer War.

When to go

All year round as this is a moderate highveld climate. Winter may afford better game-viewing opportunities because the vegetation dies down.

Other rides

The **Two Provinces** ride offers an 84km circuit route that consists of 39km on tar and 45km on dirt. Start and finish at the Bird Store on the R560, but please note that safe parking is not guaranteed. From the Bird Store turn left onto the R560. Take the dirt road to Hartbeesfontein.

From Remhoogte turn left onto the R560. Just before the tar road makes a sharp turn into Skeerpoort, you will need to turn right onto the Hartebeeshoek dirt road that goes over the mountains. Turn right again at the T-junction onto a tar road and ride back into Gauteng past the CSIR Hartebeeshoek satellite tracking station.

At the T-junction with the R563 to Hekpoort turn left and then immediately right onto the next dirt road to Orient. After 9km turn right at the Magaliesburg sign. From there it is a lovely rollercoaster of a ride into the village via Valley Lodge

HOW TO PACE YOURSELF ON AN OFF-ROAD RIDE

1) **You can't wait** to start the ride, but your body will need a gentle warning. Stretch out your legs, arms, neck and shoulders. If your muscles are not 'warm' you could be setting yourself up for injury.

2) **Let all the other riders** champing at the bit go off ahead of you. This is just the beginning, and it is pointless maxing out your heart rate just to try to keep up with them.

3) **Reached the first hill yet?** You will notice how you are now passing 'the warm up champions' who dropped you earlier.

4) **Invest in a heart rate monitor** – it has been likened to your body's rev-counter. Ascertain what your maximum heart rate is. On the climbs, try to keep your heart rate to 80% of max. When you recover, get it down to 60% of max.

5) **Finish the way you started,** with your stretching exercises. Cycling shortens your muscles, so stretching before and after a ride is essential to maintain suppleness.

RIGHT: The red soil of the Magaliesberg will dust both your calves and your bike.

(this section also forms part of the Brait Grace-to-Grace corporate mountain bike race). Thereafter, ride on back to the start via the Bekker Schools Road and Goblin's Cove.

The ride over **Breedtsnek** is 23km one way. Do a circuit route or return the same way. Start and finish at the Bird Store on R560, but, once again, safe parking is not guaranteed.

Ride 6km up the dirt road past Ingwe Bush Camp on your right. Follow the Magaliesberg mountains looming to the right. Keep going until you get to a T-junction. Keep turning right until the steep switchbacks announce that the nek is near. Admire the view and decide if you are going to take the long way home or head back the way you came.

The ride at **Mount Grace** is a 10km circuit route. Start and finish at the hotel. It is a tough little ride through indigenous bush full of proteas.

Test your fitness and skills along jeep tracks around the hotel property. There are also GT Avalanche bikes available to hire. Day visitors are welcome, but visits are by appointment only. (014) 577-1350

Annual mountain bike events include the Adoons MTB Classic in May that starts from the Magaliesberg Station and consists of 60/40km races. Also in May is the Magalies Monster MTB race (75/40/20km) while September welcomes the Bekker Schools Bundu Bash.

Off-the-bike entertainment

Ingwe Bush Camp also offers hunting, game viewing, team building activities and hiking.

Or go to the Mount Grace Country Hotel and Spa that lies 22km away. Pamper your mind and body with a day of luxurious health treatments at this tranquil and upmarket resort. (014) 577-1350 ext 100

The Cradle of Humankind is a mere 25km drive away. Turn off the R563 to the Sterkfontein Caves. The Magaliesberg and Kromdraai areas have the richest and oldest deposits of hominid remains in the world.

For more information, call them on (011) 957-0034 or visit www.cradleofhumankind@gpg.gov.za

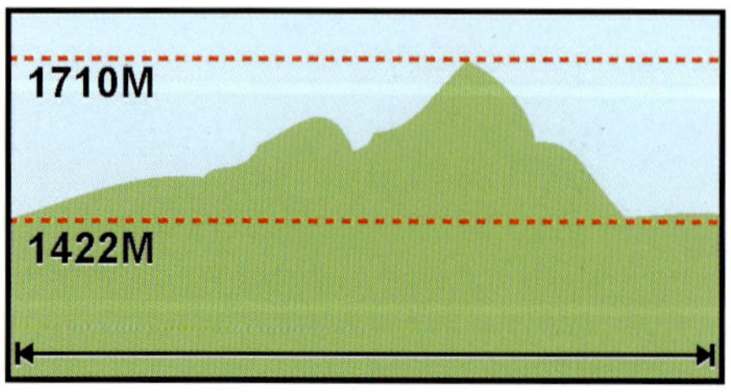

FAST FACTS

ROUTE
A circular route. Possible to lengthen the ride with several detours available. It offers a challenging return ride up a concrete road.

TRAFFIC
Virtually none, except for the occasional game-viewing vehicle that you may encounter.

ATTRACTIONS
Breathtaking 360° views (Nooitgedacht is the highest point in the Magaliesberg), with some awesome jeep track thrown in. The viewing of game at the tips of your bar-ends is guaranteed.

START POINT
Tented camp:
25°87.276' South, 27°53.124' East

FACILITIES
Overnight hospitality is offered in a well-appointed tented bush camp. Conference centre. Self or full catering options are available.

ENTRY FEE
A nominal entry fee is charged at gate.
An excellent map is also available here.

CONTACT NUMBERS
Ingwe Bush Camp: 82 449-9075
Cliff@ingwebushcamp.com
www.ingwebushcamp.com
Map info: Craig Beech at cbeech@mighty.co.za

BEWARE OF
Ingwe has an abundance of non-predatory wild animals – keep your distance so as not to disturb them.

THUMBS DOWN
It would make a great ride even better if the full extent of the routes on this property, especially the ones on the top of Nooitgedacht Mountain, was marked more clearly to direct visiting off-road cyclists.

OPPOSITE: The farm is set against the southern slopes of the Magaliesberg mountains and gentle grass plains give way to steeper slopes. The climbs that you face at Ingwe can be quite challenging, but the exceptional views and awesome jeep track more than make up for all the hard work.

392

COOLEST SINGLETRACK

Province: Western Cape Closest Town: Knysna Distance: 12–24km

...imagine a mountain bike ride as fast and free and flowing as an African river – carving in and out amongst ancient trees...

KNYSNA

Knysna is situated centrally within South Africa's renowned Garden Route, a region blessed with supreme natural splendour slumbering peacefully along the Indian Ocean. Twice nominated as South Africa's favourite town and less than 500km from Cape Town, this holiday hotspot has earned its reputation as a perennial favourite amongst both local and international tourists. Settlers originally came here to exploit vast swathes of hardwood trees and, during more than a century of unrestrained commercial logging, managed to destroy in excess of 200 000 hectares of indigenous woodland. Fortunately, the 65 000 hectares of forest which has survived is currently managed according to strict conservation principles that focus on both sustainability and regeneration.

Venture beyond these magical forests and you will soon discover a range of other natural treasures along the Garden Route – unspoilt beaches, vast freshwater lake systems, skyscraping mountain ranges, pristine marine estuaries and rivers, collectively offering a perfect mix of action and satisfaction. Harkerville, rated as the flagship trail in the area, offers mountain bikers four route options encompassing everything from an easy gravel meander to one of the most wicked singletrack rides on the planet.

PREVIOUS PAGE: Riders navigate a section of fynbos singletrack along coastal cliffs that plunge more than a hundred metres to the Indian Ocean below.
LEFT: Terrain varies from short sections of sand and tree root strips to boulder fields, but generally the surface is well compacted and suited to tight riding.

30%

DISTANCE – A moderate 12–24km

30%

TIME IN THE SADDLE – 2–3 hours

30%

DANGER – On wet days, slippery tree roots and wooden bridges make for extreme fall potential

50%

TECHNICAL LEVEL – Generally good quality jeep and singletrack surfaces; roots and a short, stony section

40%

GRADIENT – A gentle gradient! OK, there are a few hills...

40%

DIFFICULTY RATING – Moderate

Rated by Jacques Marais

The setting

Marine, coastal, fynbos, estuarine, grassland and other ecosystems vie for attention amidst the renowned Knysna forests. An expansive saltwater estuary encompasses a biologically diverse marine environment brimming with the fascinating and many creatures of the sea, including an endemic species of seahorse. Fields of fynbos, often resplendent with proteas and ericas in full bloom, form buffer zones between forests and coastal plains and blanket some of the higher-lying mountain slopes and plateaus. The nearby Goukamma Nature Reserve boasts transitional vegetation ranging from hardy fynbos scrub to thickets dense with coastal milkwood and candlewood, giving shelter to diverse species such as vervet monkey, honey badger, porcupine, water mongoose and the endangered African black oystercatcher.

In the end, the forests prevail as the jewel in the Garden Route's botanical crown, imparting a timeless and tranquil ambience where ancient yellowwood, stinkwood and hard pear trees prosper within the temperate embrace of the balmy Indian Ocean. The variety of micro-habitats makes for an impressive bird list, with 'lifers' such as the narina trogon and osprey often making an appearance. Sightings of caracal, leopard, bush pig, the ghostlike forest elephants and other mammal species may be infrequent, but their spoor is a constant reminder that they share their forest habitat with you and your bikes.

How to get there

Knysna is situated approximately 480km from Cape Town and 260km from Port Elizabeth along the coastal N2 highway. To get to the start of the Harkerville Trail, travel along the N2 for just on 20km towards Plettenberg Bay, looking out for the sign indicating the 'Garden of Eden' to the left. Obtain your permit at the Forestry Office here and crank across the road to get to the trailhead, or alternatively take the Harkerville turn-off right a few kilometres further on and follow the road to the Forestry Office.

Best rides

If you want it all in a single morning, go and ride the Harkerville Trail. Not only do the four routes offer options suited to anyone from an off-road virgin to pro riders, but the gentle topography and deep-forest fantasy feel make for a

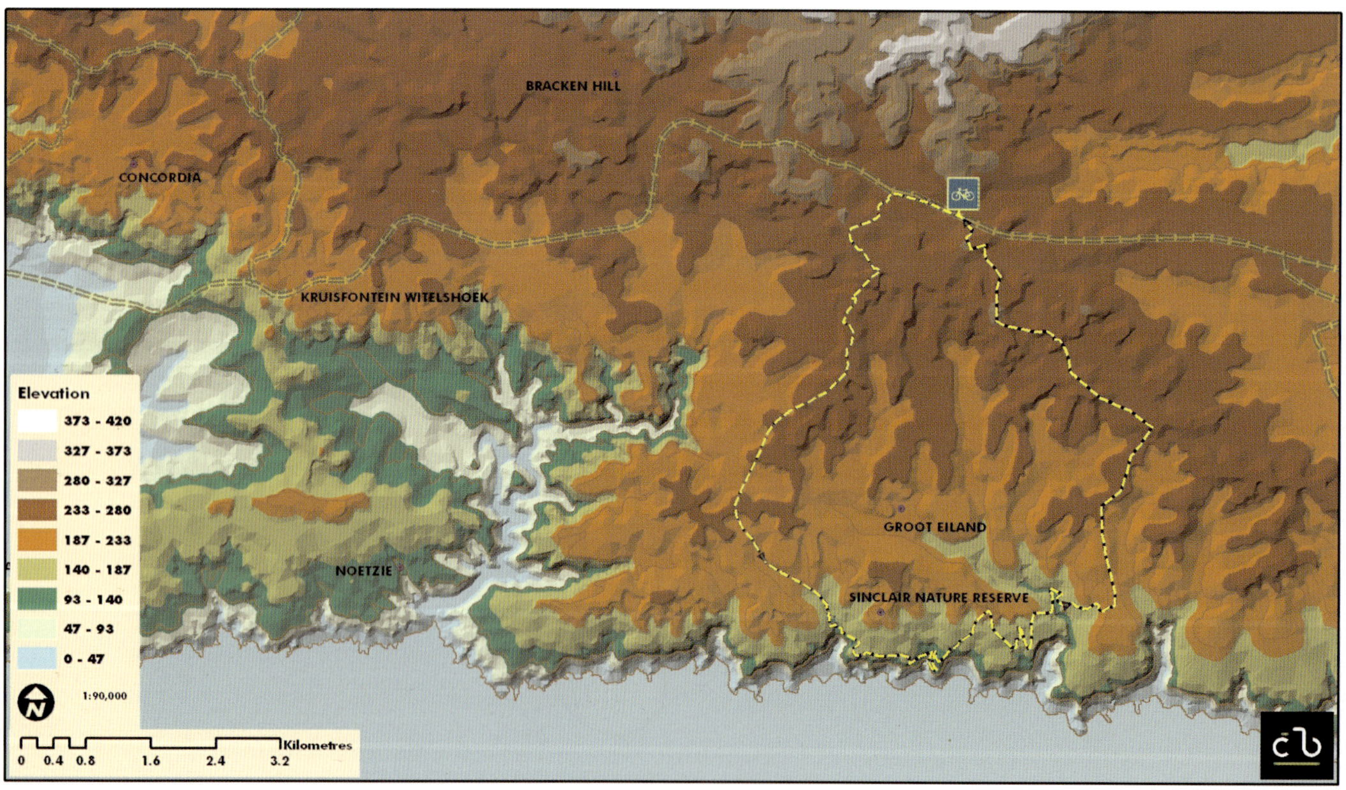

phenomenal day out. The various routes are colour coded and well marked to ensure a smooth riding experience, allowing you to choose between gravel road meanders, cliff-hugging mountain trails, pedal-to-the-metal singletrack and hard core downhill blasts.

You have four routes to choose from, of which the **Yellow Route** is the only trail you can ride in wet conditions. This 14km circular route is limited to good quality gravel roads, thus offering an easy and reasonably level route the whole family will enjoy (riding time is just over an hour). Although the 12km **Blue Route** is a tad shorter, it incorporates a 2.5km section of singletrack (the Forestry guys refer to this as a slip road) along Beukespad, thus markedly upping the endorphin rush and required skills level. Expect to spend around an hour and a half in the saddle as you cruise along in the shade of typical medium-high forest – and don't miss the patch of soaring redwoods dating back to 1927. Next up is the 15km **Green Route** with a riding time of just over two hours. You could easily turn this ride into a full-day affair by incorporating an additional coastal loop along fynbos-covered cliffs before cooling off at the shady swimming hole along Waterpad Road.

Top of most riders' To Do lists will be the spectacular **Red Route** and there is absolutely no excuse why even rookie riders should shy away from the biking bliss awaiting them along this superb trail. Combine the hypnotic curve and swerve of singletrack with swooping service roads, set it down within a tranquil, deep-forest environment and throw in a few breathtaking coastal stretches and you get what arguably rates as South Africa's favourite mountain bike ride.

The Red Route kicks off across the highway from the entrance to the Garden of Eden, but forestry officials prefer mountain bikers to use the parking at the Harkerville Forestry

BELOW: Take care when negotiating wooden bridges and ramps as these often become extremely slippery during wet conditions in the forest.

Office further down the N2 towards Plettenberg Bay. Start off at the trailhead on the Grooteilandpad T-junction and follow the faint singletrack along the southern edge of the N2, dipping through the concrete irrigation channel twice before dog-legging left (1km) to ascend into the forest. Cruise into the emerald gloom along a gentle singletrack climb before negotiating the little drop-off onto Markpad (2km), where you turn right along the jeep track for a few hundred metres.

A left turn onto Beukespad takes you along a ripping slip of single and dual track meandering amongst towering trees trailing bearded moss and verdant stands of seven year ferns. Dodge the piles of bush pig poo and fallen branches until you meet up with the Markpad again (5.5km), then turn right and left again (6km) onto Olifantpad. Batten down into an absolute dream of a ride as you slope away towards the coast, taking care along the occasional stream crossing (watch out for the descent towards the second creek at the 9km mark, where you can fill up your water bottles).

A sharp little climb kicks in towards the Gumbelt, but soon flattens out as you burst into fynbos country (11km) with stunning views across the rugged Indian Ocean coastline. Sections of the trail here have been given a concrete surface and you might be tempted to feed on speed as you bang down to what must be one of the most beautiful picnic spots on the planet (12km).

Take a breather, eat a biscuit, slug a swig of magic potion and then hit the downhill before rattling every bone in your body along a rocky section of trail before you swoop down onto a bridge crossing along a steep gravel road (14km). This is a good spot to grab a swim on those sweltering summer days, especially as there is a stiff climb lurking en route to where you rejoin the Green Route (15.5km).

Huff and puff onto the Waterpad (you could follow the alternative Green Route loop off to your right towards the coast again) before turning left after a few hundred metre). Crank into a few steep and exposed sections of Kleineilandpad, climbing along a cleared section until you re-enter the forest after approximately 2km. Turn left onto Perdekoppad (19km) to whack into a brief stretch of singletrack before blasting onto Geelstootpad (21km), a narrow gravel service road connecting you onto the *pièce de résistance* of this rollicking ride.

The final free-ride section of the Red Route super-tubes along a zigzag descent to carve in and out amongst the swish of tree ferns then crosses a boardwalk bridge, goes up a steep embankment before ducking below a gnarled trunk to where you dismount at the Downhill Tree to give thanks for the ride of a lifetime (24km).

ABOVE: Easily negotiable drop-offs add to the exhilaration of this fast-paced and flowing ride.
OPPOSITE: Once you leave the forest behind, stunning vistas open up across the Indian Ocean.

In my book, the Harkerville Red Route offers everything a mountain biker could look for, so saddle up and zone into the zen of mountain biking meditation. And, as they say in the classics, that's not all – Petrus-se-Brand, Homtini, Diepwalle and a multitude of other trails are waiting to be explored.

When to go

Knysna boasts a temperate climate with an annual rainfall varying between 850 and 1 000mm. Temperatures vary from a summer average of 27°C to a median of around 15°C during the cooler winter months, thus making the town an ideal year-round family getaway.

The riding is good all year round, but be aware that many of the trails may be closed during wet weather for both ecological and safety reasons.

Off-the-bike entertainment

Knysna during the holiday season gets really busy with both local and foreign visitors flocking here. Many folk also do enjoy the tourist crush during the winter festival months.

But it is outside school and public holidays that the true nature of this delightful town shines through. The locals are more relaxed, it is easy to find parking, prices drop down to an affordable rand level and there is no sign of rush hour along the mountain biking trails.

If you're keen on some time out of the saddle, you had better start prioritising in order to get around to the diverse range of action and leisure options awaiting you. Anything goes, from fly-fishing the estuary, abseiling off the craggy Knysna Heads or kayaking the breathtaking coastline to dolphin-watching from a paraglider and horse riding along the remote beaches. Not to be missed is the annual Knysna Oyster Festival held in July, a trip on the Outeniqua Choo-Tjoe steam train and a solo escape into the emerald silence of the indigenous forests.

HOW TO SURVIVE WET TERRAIN

1) **Close call** – when a trail has been closed by forestry officials, they have done so for a reason. Save yourself a potentially dangerous wipe-out by opting to ride one of the other trails.

2) **Crud catcher** – install a mud guard or compact crud-catcher strip to stop mud from your front wheel splattering up into your face and blinding you.

3) **Shed tread** – fit tyres suited to muddy conditions. The tread pattern should be aggressive and able to shed mud before a build-up accumulates, thus ensuring you of constant traction.

4) **Bridge too far** – wet bridges and boardwalks equal Holiday on Ice. Approach crossings straight-on and do not attempt to brake if you're keen to survive with your pride (and skin) intact.

5) **Washing well** – save yourself heaps of time by washing your bike as soon as you get home. Once you have removed the mud, immediately apply lube to your chain and all moving parts to repell moisture.

OPPOSITE: Giant tree ferns splay across a deep-forest section of the Harkerville Red Route singletrack.
ABOVE: Although the occasional push might be called for, most cyclists will find Harkerville an enjoyable ride.

FAST FACTS

ROUTE
The Harkerville Trail consists of four route options of varying degrees of difficulty.

TRAFFIC
Mostly other mountain bikers bombing down the trail; also look out for hikers along certain sections.

ATTRACTIONS
Magic forests and beach hikes, a creative and vibey community, swimming with dolphins, oysters.

START POINT
Harkerville trailhead:
34°02.310' South, 23°14.311' East

FACILITIES
Water, ablutions, maps and reasonably secure parking at the Harkerville Forestry Office.

ENTRY FEE
A very nominal fee is payable to obtain a mountain bike permit.

CONTACT NUMBERS
Mountain Biking Africa Safaris: 082 783-8392
arcent@mweb.co.za
Knysna Tourism: (044) 382-5510
knysna.tourism@pixie.co.za
Map info: Craig Beech at cbeech@mighty.co.za

BEWARE OF
High annual rainfall can cause severely slippery conditions, especially in the forest.

THUMBS DOWN
Full marks to the Forestry Department on this one. Unfortunately, any rainy or wet conditions will relegate you to riding on jeep track and gravel roads yet again.

LEFT: Harkerville's deep-forest fantasy feel makes for a phenomenal day out.
OPPOSITE: Ocean views, forest singletrack, sunshine – at 12km into the ride, what more could a mountain biker want?

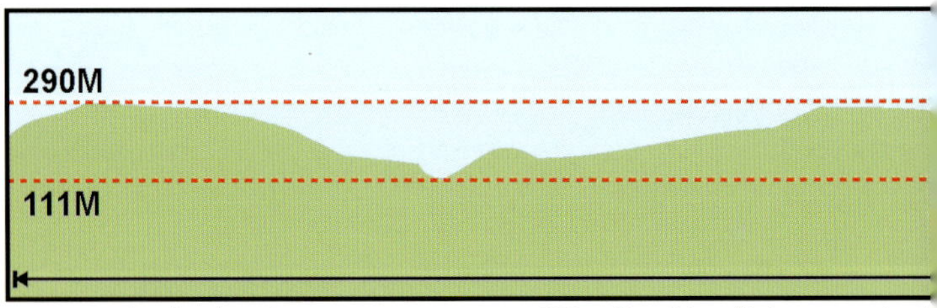

Warning: Harkerville's dense forest cover prevents accurate GPS tracking. This profile is an approximati

MOST ALL-ROUND EPIC

Province: Free State Closest Town: Marquard Distance: 30km

...blaze your way across the plateau over exposed sheets of rock, through mountain streams and along singletrack created by the resident mad cows.

KORANNA

Should you find yourself in need of relaxation, go and experience the expanse of the Free State and replenish your soul. Once acquainted, you will return again and again to savour those big skies and eternal landscapes. People doing the 'redeye' drive between Johannesburg and Cape Town wrongly assume the Free State to be a monotonous pancake of sunflower and mielie fields, punctuated by the occasional windmill and lonely farmhouse. Those intrepid enough to divert just a little east of the N1 highway will be pleasantly surprised by the sight of solitary sandstone buttresses thrusting up in defiance of the plains. Get to the top of one of these, and you can see forever.

The Koranna mountains are a weekend escape for stressed twenty-first century city dwellers, just as they were a refuge for fleeing tribes in the seventeenth century. In 1775 the Kora tribe moved into this area. The Korannas, as they became known, were still living in this area when the first white settlers arrived. Later it was occupied by Magul, a cannibal who lived in a cave, during and after the time of Shaka's reign.

In 1985, the anthropological and natural resources of the Koranna were recognised, and the 7 000 hectare Koranna Conservancy was established to protect them. Five years later, the Marquard Business Association and Johannesburg Mountain Bicycle Club initiated SA's first official mountain biking trail.

PREVIOUS PAGE: Cycling up the second mountain is a mission. A rest at 'Magul se Gat' can be combined with a swim in the nearby dam, though there is little time for such diversions on the Koranna Two Mountains MTB Classic, held in spring every year.
LEFT: From the top of Widow's Hill you can see forever with the mountains of Lesotho in the distance.

50%

DISTANCE – A tough 30km

70%

TIME IN THE SADDLE – 4–5 hours (incl. 1 hour for Widow's Hill)

60%

DANGER – Extreme heat or cold, thorns

60%

TECHNICAL LEVEL – Some tricky riding here

90%

GRADIENT – Very steep

70%

DIFFICULTY RATING – A tough ride that will weed out the genuine from the 'image is critical' types

Rated by Herman Mills

The setting

Flat-topped mountains with dappled sheer sandstone cliffs covered in scratchy scrub bush with clusters of duiwel thorns that lurk off the beaten track. Long grass thats caresses your legs and wets your shoes with dew.

Cow pats, bumpy hoof prints, and the smell of cattle pervade the air. Sandstone fence posts and old broken walls. Barbed wire fences and farm gates, each with an individual hand-wound wire catch to twist and turn like a Rubik cube puzzle. This is the landscape that awaits you in these mountains of the Free State.

How to get there

From Johannesburg, take the N1 south to Bloemfontein. Just before Winburg, look for the 'Stasie' sign and turn right onto this road. Turn left onto the N5 to Senekal, and 2.5km later turn right onto the R708 to Marquard and Clocolan.

Travel for about 35km, looking for farm road S111 on the right. Travel 25km down this road, past Table Mountain. Cross over the bridge and 1km further you will see signs to Merrimetsie on the left. The unmistakable Koranna mountains loom straight ahead of you.

The ride

Initially, you will be riding along the foot of the Koranna mountains, roughly parallel to the Klein Vet River. There are sweeping views to the left, across the river valley towards Flora, Commissioner's Flat and Table Mountain. To the right lies the Magermanshoek farm, nestled in the cleavage of the two mountains. This section passes very quickly as it is flat and on a well-used hard-pack dirt road. After a steep, gnarly crossing through the dip of a perennial spruit (watch out that you're in the right gear and don't stall), the Van Zoelenshoek farm and its cattle pens will be in sight. Keep going straight along the foot of the mountain. Almost immediately all conversation will die, as the gradient starts to consume your lungs and legs, thereby announcing the commencement of Widow's Hill. Initially, riders are permitted the grace of a few sections for recovery, but this is a supremely difficult 5km climb and, when you attempt it, you will respect its formidable reputation amongst mountain bikers. The last 3km are merciless, with all but the most elite riders off their bikes, ruefully admiring the view.

The top of Widow's Hill is by no means the top, and it's a series of gradual ascents ever higher up and over the plateau

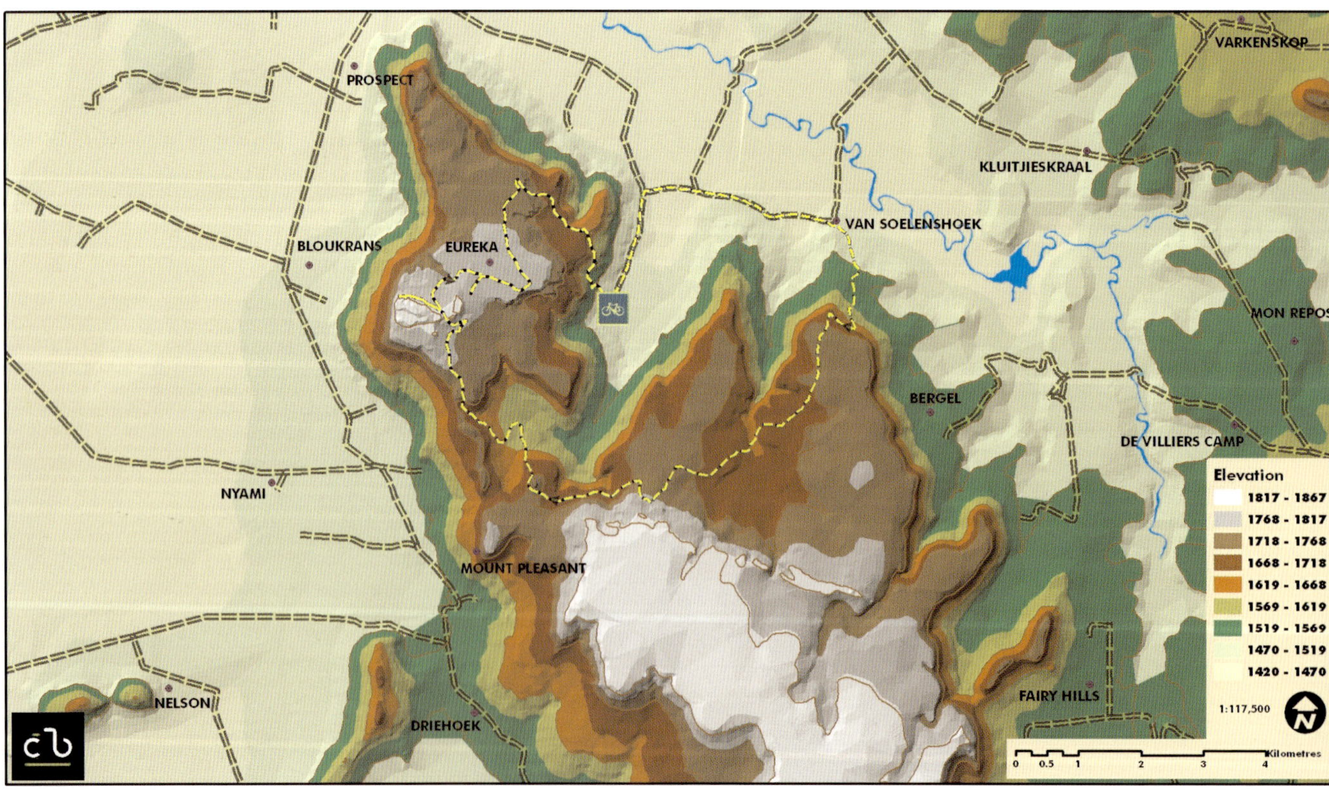

of the first mountain. This is mountain bike riding at its best as you blaze your way across the plateau over exposed sheets of rock, through mountain streams and along the singletrack created by the resident mad cows. Leading up to Jonas van Tonder se Plek, the highest point on this ride, you will be cycling along jeep tracks which unmercifully hammer your backside and scratch your legs since they are covered in knobs of tough plateau grasses and fynbos. Thereafter, a singletrack spits you out onto a steep section of exposed rock which is rideable the whole way down... if you choose the correct line. This is followed by a fast singletrack to a portage over a stile and then grassy plateau begins to give way to rocky slopes as you head towards a prominent rocky knoll. The view from here will simply blow away any presumptions you ever had about the Free State.

From here, the descent down the first mountain into Magermanshoek begins in earnest. After going around the back of a knoll consisting of huge boulders, the trail narrows until you are contemplating in disbelief the sheer cliff you are about to descend. Called 'derailleurs' demise' because of competitive riders' habit of throwing their bikes down here during an annual race, remember that you are here to enjoy the ride, so a little bit of teamwork is called for. Send one rider down to grab and stash the bikes that another eases down the cliff. From here you are likely to be on and off the bike, dodging rocks until the singletrack becomes too rocky and steep and loose for you to stay in the saddle. A bit later, there's nice riding as the slope rolls out through some dongas. At this point, the riders who were complaining up Widow's Hill will be crying for home, and the ride can be shortened here with a rolling jeep track downhill (interrupted by a few farm gates) past Magermanshoek homestead and then straight back to Merrimetsie.

Now the climb up the second mountain begins, and it is the same story as Widow's Hill, with two small differences: a) it is not as long, and b) near the end, it is excessively steep. Breathless at the top, you will see the plateau grassland is quite pristine and not as heavily utilised as that of the first mountain. If you are not too tired, you can get into a good rhythm and cover this section fast. On the first mountain, the view is basically behind you as you ride – on the second mountain, it is all-encompassing. As you begin to come off the plateau, you are cowed to insignificance by the huge sandstone rock formations that stand like sentinels along the jeep track. Those with a fetish for churning the big ring and pumping adrenaline will not be looking around them at this stage: they'll be too busy throwing the bike about and having a buzz. Suddenly the jeep track is on open ground as you approach the lip of the radical descent to Merrimetsie. This is the infamous 'Death Cookie Downhill', and your bike feels like it's skittering over marbles with a mind of its own and you fear losing control into the grim clusters of loose rocks that line the track. You either go very fast, or very slowly down here – both can have disastrous consequences! Without warning, you are back on the road past Magermanshoek in a haze of bike-induced ecstacy.

When to go

In September, if good rains have fallen early, there are lots of beautiful spring flowers and greenery. It gets hot here in summer, October to April, with clouds of flies and mosquitoes; cold and dry in winter, May to August, with temperatures falling below 0°C. Firethorn bushes festoon the winter mountains in garlands of red and orange berries.

Other rides

Rietfontein Ride lies 12km outside Marquard on the other side of the railway line. Self-catering accommodation for six guests is available in a well-appointed annexe to the beautiful sandstone farmhouse where fish fossils can be seen in the hewn rock walls. The bush here is harsh and infamous for its legions of thorns. Puncture-proof your tyres or else you will have to walk. Rietfontein is a working farm and a map will be supplied to riders to explore it all by bicycle. Guided walks can also be arranged to view dinosaur footprints. There is a swimming pool to cool off in afterwards during the hot summer months. (051) 991-7048 after hours

St Augustines is 67km from Marquard. Previously an extensive mission station, dating back to the early 1800s, it is still run by the Anglican Church. Guests come here for conferences and spiritual retreat. There are five religious sites here, among them a cave where the first missionaries lived, Bushman paintings and an interesting graveyard. There is also a fascinating library with many antique books. Guests and day visitors are welcome to bring their bicycles and ride a 25km farm road route. Follow the Modderpoort railway line along the S513, turning left over the mountain on the S36 into Ladybrand. After stopping for tea and cake in town, take the S7 parallel to the railway line out of Ladybrand and back to St Augustines. (051) 924-3318

HOW TO RIDE DOWN ROCKY JEEP TRACK

There are two lovely terms for rocks in MTB lingo: 'Death cookies': biscuit-size rocks that make you feel like you are riding on ball bearings, and 'Baby heads': get the bike away from their nursery as these little guys would love to meet you. Here are some pointers on how to deal with rocks in a downhill situation.

1) **'Eyes ahead.'** Never look just in front of your front wheel – the sight could terrify you! Keep your eyes ahead so that you can anticipate what the terrain is going to throw at you and select the best line to point your bike through it.

2) **Hang loose** and go with the flow. The harder you grip those brakes and stiffen up on the bike, the less control you will have of your trusty steed.

3) **Keep your weight back** and off the front wheel. Chances are that if the front wheel makes it over a rut or loose rock, you and the rest of the bike will follow through like an express train.

So, the key to riding a rocky downhill is not necessarily all about speed, but how smoothly you can ride it...

Off-the-bike entertainment

In and around Koranna and Merrimetsie you'll find hiking, 4x4 trails, a quad biking trail, abseiling, bird watching, as well as guided walks to view Bushman paintings and some Listrosaurus tracks.

Marquard is the hub town of Sparta Beef with 50 000 head of cattle on farms all around the town. If you love red meat, don't miss a visit to BJ's Butchery in town. To avoid disappointment, do bring cash as there is no credit card facility out here.

There is an upgraded nine hole golf course and a renovated clubhouse, for those who like to hit 'the flying white dammit'.

Trips to asparagus and cherry farms can be arranged, and don't miss viewing the town's beautiful Dutch Reformed sandstone church, built in 1926 and designed by architects Louw and Moerdyk. A monument of stones to commemorate the Great Trek was erected in 1938 and can still be seen at the church today. A mysterious message from the last century is pledged to be excavated from this monument in 2038.

RIGHT: The climb up Widow's Hill is formidable. Pace yourself and take your mind off the terrain ahead by looking at the view.

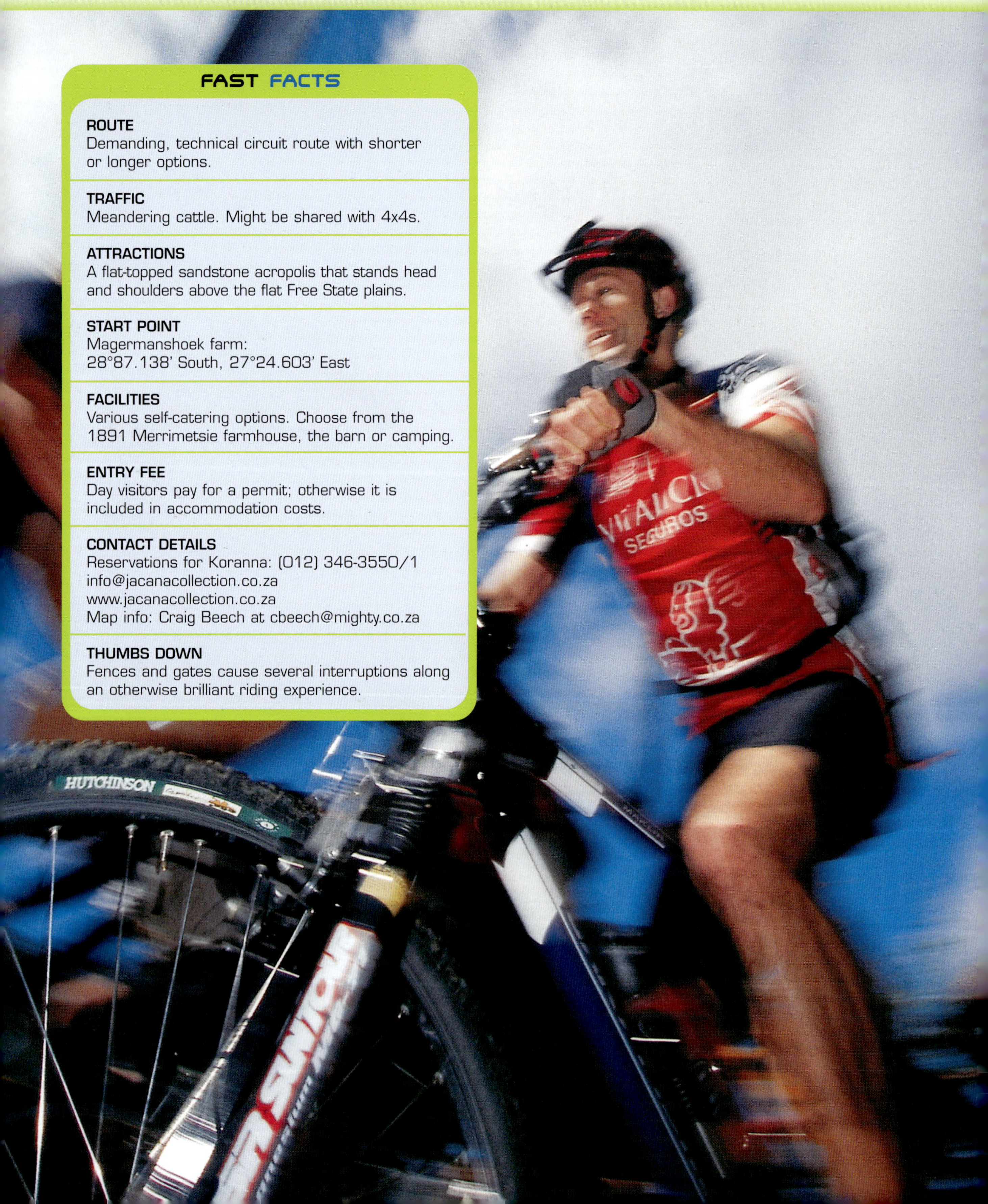

FAST FACTS

ROUTE
Demanding, technical circuit route with shorter or longer options.

TRAFFIC
Meandering cattle. Might be shared with 4x4s.

ATTRACTIONS
A flat-topped sandstone acropolis that stands head and shoulders above the flat Free State plains.

START POINT
Magermanshoek farm:
28°87.138' South, 27°24.603' East

FACILITIES
Various self-catering options. Choose from the 1891 Merrimetsie farmhouse, the barn or camping.

ENTRY FEE
Day visitors pay for a permit; otherwise it is included in accommodation costs.

CONTACT DETAILS
Reservations for Koranna: (012) 346-3550/1
info@jacanacollection.co.za
www.jacanacollection.co.za
Map info: Craig Beech at cbeech@mighty.co.za

THUMBS DOWN
Fences and gates cause several interruptions along an otherwise brilliant riding experience.

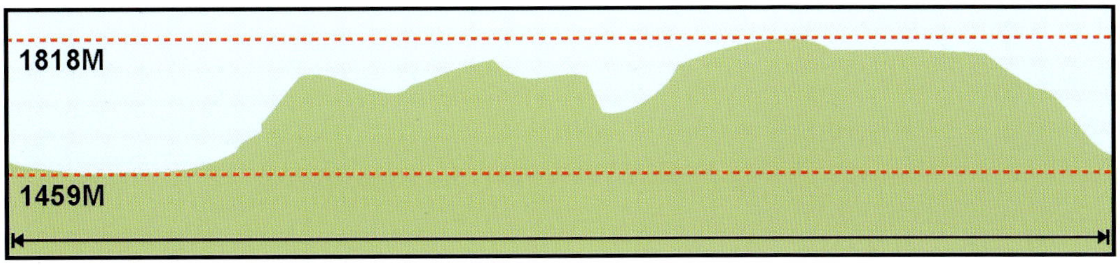

OPPOSITE: The Koranna Two Mountains MTB Classic is renowned for its variety of course conditions which test both skills and fitness. ABOVE: Look out for balancing marble rocks – some of the striking formations on this trail.

WILDEST RIDE

Province: Mpumalanga **Closest Town:** Phalaborwa **Distance:** 21.4km

The gentle terrain allows your attention to be focused on your African wilderness experience...

KRUGER

The size of a small country, the Kruger National Park is South Africa's flagship reserve and ranks amongst the world's greatest conservation areas. Originally proclaimed in 1898 by President Paul Kruger, it now comprises 1 948 528 hectares, is 350km long and measures 90km at its widest point. Stretching from Zimbabwe in the north, it follows the natural border of the Lebombo Mountains of Mozambique. On its western flanks the park straddles both the Mpumalanga and Limpopo provinces. Private game farms and upmarket lodges abound between the Kruger Park and the northern ranges of the Drakensberg Mountains.

Perhaps because of its monolithic size, the Kruger Park did not adopt ecotourism activities as quickly as the newer (sometimes very expensive) private concerns that are clustered around its borders. Childhood memories of many Kruger visitors may have been of hours sitting cooped up in a car, eagerly scanning the bush for a glimpse of some reclusive wild animal, but eventually succumbing to boredom and fighting with siblings on the back seat. All that has changed in the last decade, as park authorities have taken tentative steps in the direction of ecotourism by introducing open vehicle game drives from the camps, followed by guided walks and, more recently, as of 4 September 2003, guided mountain bike rides.

PREVIOUS PAGE: Olifants Camp on the banks of the Olifants River is the departure point for the guided mountain bike trails.
LEFT: Sunsets in the Kruger National Park are legendary for their clarity and beauty.

30%
DISTANCE – A short 21.4km

40%
TIME IN THE SADDLE – 4 hours of game viewing

50%
DANGER – Chance encounters with hippo, elephant or lion

20%
TECHNICAL LEVEL – Easy rocky hard-pack surface

10%
GRADIENT – Only one short, steep incline on the return ride

30%
DIFFICULTY RATING – Easy

Rated by Herman Mills

The setting

So as not to spoil the experience of other tourists in the park (who may be astounded at seeing a mountain biker weaving in and out of the mopane trees) the rides take place well away from where visitors in motor vehicles are viewing game. On a bicycle, one can cover much greater distances than on foot and access parts of the reserve that are rarely seen. If apprehensive about a bicycle safari on the wild side amongst the big five in the Kruger, just consider it in the light of human density at its worst – rush hour traffic in any major city – and you may well agree that the bicycle safari is safer by far! Mountain biking will generate much needed income for conservation. The project might be extended to other camps, with Mopane Rest Camp and the five bushveld camps as possible venues. The idea of cycling in the Kruger Park was pioneered by one of the Park's rangers, Hein Grobler: 'In 1999 the idea was to start mountain bike trails in the Kruger National Park. I started this project and it was initially going to be launched at Bateleur Bushveld Camp, in the far-northern region. When I was transferred to Olifants Camp, the project came with me. Finally, after many proposals, the project was approved.'

How to get there

Visitors must ensure they reach the entry gates in good time. Camp and reserve entry gates close at 17h30 in winter and 18h30 in summer. Latecomers will not be allowed in until the next day. No matter which direction you are travelling from, all facilities and roads in the park are very well signposted. Quality maps are available at the entry gates.

The ride

The name 'Hardekool Draai' originated from a huge leadwood tree (*Combretum imberbi*) that grows on the banks of the nearby Olifants River. From Olifants Camp cyclists travel in an open game-viewing vehicle with their field guide, in a westerly direction on the main road (H1-5) for 12km. A specially manufactured Venter trailer transports the bicycles behind the vehicle. The Hardekool Draai Trail starts with a pre-ride briefing by your field guide amongst typical mopane vegetation on a jeep track in total wilderness. Since youare now a second-class citizen in big five territory, it is imperative that you pay attention to the instructions of your guide and follow them without question. It could save your life if you get on the wrong side of a wild animal.

This ride is a gentle one over a slightly rocky ranger's road that doubles as a firebreak. Anywhere off this track, the ground is carpeted with a huge variety of thorns. (Hence the emphasis is on using the camp's bikes, not your own.) Although Hardekool Draai may rate as a 'novice ride' in some cyclist's classification, it has been selected because the concept behind the Kruger Park rides is all about integration with what surrounds you – from the smallest insect to the largest animal.

This can be a tricky balance to maintain for, the more you cycle, the more you become engrossed in the ride, forgetting all about the appreciation of your surroundings. The gentle terrain of Hardekool Draai therefore allows your attention to be focused on enhancing your African wilderness experience.

Your field guide has been trained to facilitate this by stopping to discuss or identify plants, animals and spoor, all the while maintaining control over his group of cycling guests. The trail leads through mopane veld, with an occasional view of the Olifants River. After a 5km warm-up, it is time to walk one of the 'wild highways' intersecting the road – tidy little paths designed by the instincts and created by the footwork of wild creatures going to and from the river.

A short diversion down to the river on foot will have any wildlife enthusiast excited.

BELOW: The Olifants/Letaba River Confluence MTB Trail runs, as its name suggests, between the Letaba River on your left and the Olifants River on your right.

LEFT: Coming across a zebra herd is part of the experience.
TOP: At the camp, birds can be viewed at close quarters.
BOTTOM: Hyena and mountain bike tracks combine.

HOW TO GO GAME VIEWING BY BIKE

1) **Do not wear** any items of clothing that are in stark contrast to your surroundings. Leave last season's neon pink lycra at home and your favourite white MTB classic T-shirt in the rondavel. Unnatural colours make wild game nervous and they will run off.

2) **Keep very quiet.** In a wilderness area sound carries for miles. Garrulous cyclists can ruin game-viewing opportunities for the rest of the group.

3) **If a wild animal** charges you, try not to panic. Obey your field guide implicitly.

4) **Never pedal away** like a lone ranger on any of these rides – stick to the protection of the pack.

FAST FACTS

ROUTE
A flat return route along stony jeep track, with small skirmishes along game paths.

TRAFFIC
None, but there could be something unexpected on intersecting 'wild' highways.

ATTRACTIONS
Uninterrupted views of the Olifants River and surrounding plains of mopane bush.

START POINT
Olifants Camp:
24°01.315 South, 31°64.957 East

FACILITIES
Olifants Camp will provide good quality mountain bikes, backpacks, water bottles, bicycle helmets and snacks. Should participants bring their personal bicycles, proof of a recent service by an accredited bicycle shop must be produced. Such participants are required to take all their own puncture repair equipment.

ENTRY FEE
There is a fee to be paid for this ride in addition to the park entry fees.

CONTACT NUMBERS
Central reservations for SANPARKS:
(012) 428-9111 or directly with
Olifants Camp two days in advance:
(013) 735-6606/7
Map info: Craig Beech at cbeech@mighty.co.za

BEWARE OF
Age before beauty – no persons under 16 years are permitted on the mountain bike trails.

THUMBS DOWN
Although it would add to the expense of this experience, it would be most reassuring to have a discreet backup vehicle following the bicycles on this ride, in addition to the armed field guides.

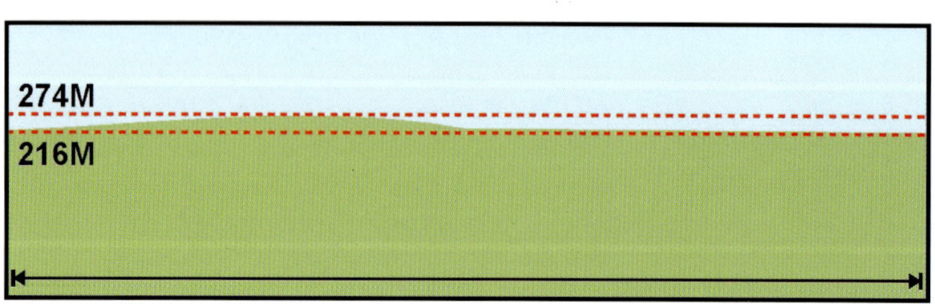

Then back to the bikes and the trail continues for 5–6km over rocky terrain, superb for mountain biking. Suddenly, you turn south onto a small hippo path where, after a few hundred metres, you will naturally drop down onto the wide banks of the Olifants River. Here you may encounter elephant so close that you can smell them and hear them eating.

Enjoy sumptuous snacks under a huge sycamore fig tree, while watching the hippo wallowing in the pools below. There are plenty of crocodile, elephant, buffalo and general game in this area, but it is the bird life along this river that is outstanding. The closing 10.7km back to the vehicle is nearly all downhill. This allows you plenty of opportunity to savour the closing moments of this amazing experience.

This ride is a tactile overload that will make a major deposit into your spiritual bank account.

When to go

Lying in a subtropical climate, this park is best visited during winter when it is cool, and easier to spot game.

Other rides

There is a 12.2km ride offered from the Olifants Camp – the **Olifants/Letaba River Confluence MTB Trail**. Drive by game-viewing vehicle northeast from Olifants Camp to the Vutamolelo Road, which is not accessible except to cyclists. On the S44 gravel road along the Olifants River, beyond the Olifants River viewpoint, an unmarked two-track road 10.3km from camp leads to an unforgettable off-road experience. The engine dies and the silence of the bush envelops you as you drink in the best scenery of the Kruger Park. Cycle between the Letaba River on your left and the Olifants River on your right, loose rocks and branches reminding you to concentrate on your line. For 6.1km along the rocky outcrops of the region, you can expect elephant, buffalo, lion, nyala, water buck, giraffe, zebra, klipspringer and impala, to name but a few of the park's 147 mammal species. The area is rich in bird life (507 species) and is a botanist's paradise (336 tree species) with plenty of opportunity to marvel at the giant baobab trees common to this area. Enjoy your breakfast packs at the confluence of these two large rivers while watching crocodiles the size of submarines feasting on fish in the rapids below. The timeless call of the fish eagle will soothe your soul and, with the grunts of hippo in the background, this is an African river symphony you will never forget. An hour or two of full bush interpretation follows, as you walk with your armed guides along the river banks before starting the 6km cycle back to the vehicle. The trip is not really strenuous, but participants should be experienced riders in order to be able to appreciate it fully.

The 24.8km **Klipkoppies Mozambique Border Trail** goes right up to the Mozambican border, a mere 22.2km from the Olifants Camp. At around 9.8km north of the camp on the S44 route past the Olifants River view point, you drive across the Letaba River on a firebreak road. Here you get on your bike in the early morning light and ride straight into the sunrise for 9.6 km. At this time of the morning, the opportunities for chance encounters with game abound. At a fork in the road, the guides will lead you southeast for 2.8km to the Lebombo Mountains and the border between South Africa and Mozambique.

Enjoy some snacks on a hill overlooking the Olifants River in the distance with Mozambique to the east. Be daring and put your hand through the fence to touch foreign soil before you cycle back down to the Letaba River, enjoying the wonderful vista of unspoilt wilderness all the way back to the vehicle.

Off-the-bike entertainment

The Olifants Camp is perched high on a rocky outcrop and overlooks the Olifants River. Book for a guided night drive or an afternoon walk – it's a treat. Bring your binoculars for long, peaceful hours that can be spent reading, napping or viewing game by the river far below. Bird-watching opportunities are amazing in this camp – many birds are so accustomed to guests that they almost eat out of your hand. Unfortunately, the baboons and monkeys are also pretty tame, and this is why all the fridges are turned back to front, and the pantry cupboards have locks.

Rondavels are basic, self-catering units, but, if you don't feel like cooking, there is an à la carte restaurant or a kiosk for meals and snacks. Remember to bring appropriate bush clothing, insect repellent, practical footwear, a big sun hat, sunblock lotion and any personal medication you may require. The guides carry a first aid kit as well as a hand-held radio for communication with base camp, in case of an emergency.

BELOW: Nowhere else in the world are you able to study these giant herbivores 'by cycle'.

BEST RAMBLE

Province: KwaZulu-Natal **Closest Town:** Howick **Distance:** 40km

The beauty of gentle, rolling green hills so characteristic of the KwaZulu-Natal Midlands is only surpassed by the creativity of the individually hand-crafted goods on offer...

MIDLANDS

For the most part, the nature of shopping has changed significantly in the last few decades. The friendly greengrocer or hardware shop down the street has mostly been replaced by soulless, high security 'convenient' shopping centres. And, inside every door you walk through, price tags reflect the exorbitant rents that retailers have to pay.

Or, sadder still, you could go to the same mall all your life, and not one shopkeeper would ever know your name. You are just part of the anonymous crowd daily milling down the walkways. And then we haven't even mentioned the horrific parking problems, the long queues and even longer faces at the pay points, or the traffic jams getting in and out of these shopping centres.

If you have been looking for that personal touch and the human element (or, more likely, a way to lure your non-biking partner away from the city), may we suggest that you pack your bags and bicycles and head to KwaZulu-Natal where you can regain the simple pleasure of browsing through handmade wares on the Midlands Meander.

PREVIOUS PAGE: One of the other attractions of the Midlands, the Midmar Dam and its infamous Mile swim offer a great cross-training opportunity.
LEFT: The Caversham Mill Bridge has an old world charm of its own.

50%
DISTANCE – 40km

50%
TIME IN THE SADDLE – 3–5 hours

20%
DANGER – High speed downhills

10%
TECHNICAL LEVEL – Smooth hard-pack and tar

50%
GRADIENT – Steep climbs are short, long climbs are gradual

30%
DIFFICULTY RATING – Moderate

Rated by Herman Mills

The setting

The Midlands Meander breathes life back into the joy of shopping. It is in complete contrast to the incongruities of city life. The beauty of gentle, rolling green hills so characteristic of the KwaZulu-Natal Midlands is only surpassed by the beauty of individually hand-crafted goods on offer – at half the price of anything in your local mall... and the hospitality? Delicious, unique homemade food and genuine, friendly and accommodating hosts will ensure that you return again and again for years to come.

There is a sense of supporting the 'right' people here, that your money is going directly to where it counts – into the community. You interact directly with the people who actually make the goods you are buying and you can witness the pride with which they display and go about their work.

How to get there

Exit off the Durban to Johannesburg N3 highway onto the R103... and stop anywhere between Mooi River and Hilton. The Midlands Meander is well signposted so you can easily decide where to stop. The really great thing about this ride is that you can start anywhere along the route.

The ride

This ride is featured for the benefit of recreational cyclists who have a penchant for rambling all day, stopping off anywhere that takes their fancy. Fast-forward cyclists, those eels in lycra, will whip around this circuit in about two hours with no stops. But cyclists who like to hit the pause button should work on around five hours. The ride is right in the heart of the Midlands Meander, and you could stop off at any venue along the way. A mixture of quiet tarred roads and well-maintained dirt roads complete a 40km round trip. Our ride started right at the top of the Meander – at Groundcover Leather Company, where the owner, Justin McCarthy, is a talented leatherworker, businessman and a mountain biking fanatic of note.

From the Groundcover parking area turn left onto the main road from Howick towards Curry's Post, passing Mulberry Hill and a variety of attractive country houses along the way. At Curry's Post stop for some refreshments at the general dealer, tucked away behind a hedge on the right. In keeping with such stores all the way up Africa, it is run and managed by several generations of a friendly, helpful family, in this case, the Desais. Here you can still buy

everything from bicycle crank sets to fish hooks, tinned food, dress patterns and candles all in one little shop, bursting at the seams. It is truly a nostalgic reminder of a sense of community that many of us never ever experienced.

Another kilometre or so, and the road turns into dirt. Keep left, where you will be rewarded with a fantastic view over the valley below and a fast but smooth downhill. Let it all hang out around the nicely cambered corners. It's tough to hit the brakes and interrupt any downhill, but a visit to Kingdom Weavers to admire their hand-woven carpets, rugs, tapestries and tableware is definitely worth slowing down for. Afterwards, carry on downhill across the busy N3 highway where motorists speed between Johannesburg and Durban oblivious to your enjoyment of the flowers, forests, bird song and fresh country air.

A long, gradual climb will take you over the next set of hills. This is a tough climb, but take the time to look back at the ever-unfolding scenery. On the inevitable fast, winding downhill your speed will easily sneak up to 70km per hour, so remember to keep it under control and go left across the bridge to Gunters. Here an ice cold draught and delicious homemade German and Swiss sausages await you. Spinning on from Gunters you will ride over a beautiful old arched bridge at Caversham Mill where the water cascades over staggered, rectangular rocks.

Don't overdo the refreshments, because after this bridge you will be cranking up a long hill with a perfect downhill

BELOW: The sections of tar road on this ride are not too busy, but keep to the left and don't relax your vigilance.

that will deposit you back onto the R103 road. This road is the major arterial of the Meander and it can get rather busy during peak season, so don't relax your vigilance.

It is worth noting that further up the R103 towards Nottingham Road, there is a superb example of a bike- and walkway, where you are safe from traffic thanks to a serious barrier. The fatalities on South Africa's roads could be significantly reduced with more such networks of pedestrian and bicycle ways. The humble bicycle is for so much more than just sport – it is a sustainable mode of personal transport.

The next stop is Out of the Blue Trading – a psychedelic feast for the eyes with a veritable riot of handmade merchandise. Your head still spinning, ride out along the tar road past a pre-World War Two iron bridge that is yet another monument to KZN's past as one of the last British colonial outposts. At the sign indicating Lion's River Trading Post, turn left along a road that is partially tar and dirt and winds through a pastoral setting.

Cross under the N3 highway again at the Curry's Post/Lion's River interchange. Here you face a hard 3km climb back up a pass to the tar road out of Howick. A left turn at the T-junction at the top of the hill will have you breathless and back at Groundcover. After some food and a rest you will be ready to explore the rest of the Meander by bike (if you are a dedicated rider).

Obviously, riding a bicycle will limit the amount of purchases you can make, so bike, busk and browse... then return in earnest the next day (with your car and wallet) to shop till you drop!

HOW TO BUILD A HYBRID BIKE FOR TOURING

1) **A 'hybrid'** is a bicycle that you can use comfortably on the road, and on undemanding off-road routes. To create a hybrid, either use your old mountain bike if you are upgrading, or look for a good second-hand bicycle.

2) A hybrid bike, particularly if you intend touring extensively, should have a **chromoly steel frame**. Steel is strong and can bear a heavy load – like the stresses of panniers with all your worldly goods, and the rider. Should the frame break in some remote outpost, you will always be able to find a welder for steel. But very few places have a tig welder for aluminium or titanium, and even fewer have ever heard of carbon fibre...

3) **Simplify!** Fit rigid forks and lose the front shocks – unless they are top-of-the-range they will be heavy, and will be yet another fussy thing to maintain or battle to find parts for.

4) **Fit the bike** with slick or semi-slick tyres. Slick tyres have less rolling resistance. They are great on tar and hard-pack, but tricky if you have to brake while off-road and impossible if you encounter sand and mud.

5) **Get comfortable:** you are going to be out there all day. Set up the hybrid bike for your body. Never skimp on your anatomy's contact points with the bike, such as your saddle, gloves for your hands and proper pedals and shoes for your feet.

6) **Add roadbike gears** (but leave the granny gear on, for those hills from hell where you can die slowly while no one's watching). The bigger gears will help you cover long distances more effectively.

When to go

September is the best month here, lovely and mild. October to April can get very hot and it often rains. May to August can get freezing cold due to the close proximity of the Drakensberg Mountains.

Other rides

Brookfield Farmhouse lies 1.5km from Hilton College. Marked routes exist on this 12-hectare farm and adjacent farms, with spectacular sweeping views towards the Karkloof and Drakensberg mountains.

Local mountain bike classic events are easily accessible from Brookfield – an ideal hospitality venue for personalised pampering after a hard ride in their luxurious B&B suites. Brookfield is synonymous with a kitchen that produces classic menus in fine country cuisine from an on-site restaurant and licensed pub. Quality, cared-for bikes are available for hire. (033) 383-0250

Glengarry Park, 30km along the Kamberg Road, is a lovely resort on the banks of the Little Mooi River where you may camp, caravan, or stay in a chalet. Fish, swim, go tubing, play golf and cycle while you're there. There's a choice of anything from 17km to 55km off-road rides in the Kamberg Valley. Routes are marked with little arrows throughout the forests around Glengarry and, if you need any more reassurance, maps are also available. (033) 267-7225

OPPOSITE: Smooth downhills like this provide welcome relief after some long, hot climbs.

Cedara, **Ferncliff** and **World's View** offer brilliant riding on extensive single and jeep tracks through working commercial forest plantations that lie on the fringes of the Pietermaritzburg suburbia. Start from Crossways or the Quarry Centre. There are no marked routes, so call upon local knowledge for your initial ride. 083 440-6764

The **Karkloof Valley** lies 12km outside Howick. With the recent formation of the Karkloof Tourism Association (KTA), exciting official biking and hiking trails are being planned in this spectacularly scenic area that will traverse both private farm and forestry properties, including the breathtaking Karkloof Falls.

Mountain biking is welcomed in the area, but bookings must be made through the KTA office. The Karkloof Country Club, where the KTA is based, provides an ideal venue to park your car and venture off into the valley on your mountain bike. (033) 330-4602

The **Rockwood Forest Lodge** offers a 20km, well-marked circuit in and around the Karkloof Nature Reserve. This ride includes some plantation roads and has one steep, rocky climb. There are many river crossings along the route and some sections of singletrack go through the indigenous Karkloof Forest.

The trail passes by two waterfalls and has some spectacular views out over the Karkloof Valley. Longer guided rides can be organised. GT hire bikes are also available. Day visitors may use the facilities by appointment only. (031) 207-3150

Just down the road from Glengarry lies the **Silverhill Guest Lodge** that offers a ride along the quiet tarred road towards Highmoor Nature Reserve.

The ride does include an 8km uphill, but soothes tired legs with beautiful scenery – and then there is the return downhill to savour. There is another short, 5km off-road ride that goes left out of the Silverhill gates, then right onto the dirt road to Dondini with a meander into valleys around Sam Properties. (033) 267-7430

There are mountain bike activities organised almost every weekend, so there are just too many 'classic' events to mention. This is what you would expect from the province that has produced South Africa's world champion downhiller, Greg Minnaar, and that has hosted the oldest MTB classic in the country, The Hilton Classic, held in Cedara Forest every year since 1989.

South African bicycle magazines carry updated event details, or point your browser to: www.maverickworld.co.za and www.kznmbc.co.za.

Off-the-bike entertainment

Apart from the featured venues encountered on the circuit, you really are spoilt for off-the-bike entertainment here. Wherever you spot the endemic Karkloof Blue butterfly, which has been adopted as the Meander icon, you are sure of a place that has something special to offer.

Peruse the full-colour, A3 brochure that is available at every outlet in the area and plan your very own expedition... there are over 400 places to choose from.

Have a look at Culamoya Chimes and, if you have children with you, don't miss Funtasy Toys, Aird Farm, Swissland Cheese and The Hobbit's Hut.

If you're looking for furniture, visit Corrie Lynn & Co, and also the Country Furniture & Décor Warehouse.

You'll find beautifully hand-woven wares at Sharrow Products and at Shuttleworth Weaving. Or, if you'd like to try your hand at flying kites, get one at Hi-Fly.

Then there are also the three spectacular waterfalls in the area: Karkloof, Howick and Woodhouse. All are well worth a visit.

OPPOSITE: The Midlands Meander breathes life back into the joy of shopping. Its gentle, rolling green hills are in stark contrast to the stress of city life. The non-threatening, good quality dirt roads make cycling here a pleasure and a ride that even novice mountain bikers will enjoy. Of course, the chocolate box scenery certainly helps to make this ride an experience not to be missed.

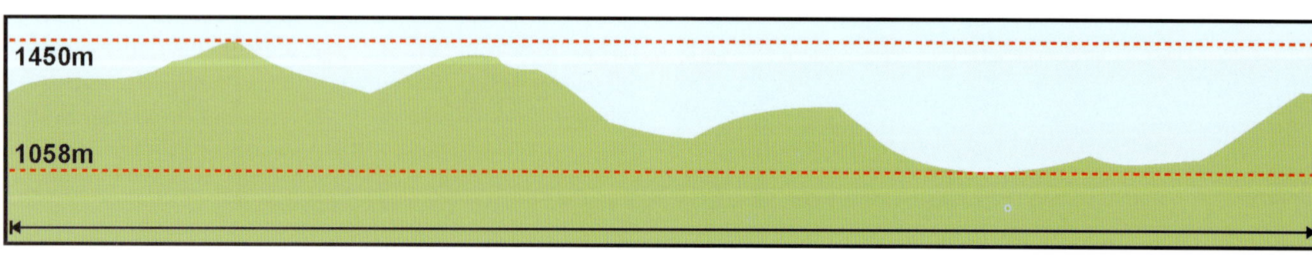

FAST FACTS

ROUTE
Circuit route on smooth dirt roads and short sections of tar.

TRAFFIC
Shared with motor vehicles.

ATTRACTIONS
Pastoral setting, with the blue spears of the Drakensberg Mountains always on the horizon.

START POINT
Groundcover Leather Company:
29°38.843' South, 30°17.560' East

FACILITIES
Just a few featured of the 400 establishments to choose from, so take your pick!

ENTRY FEE
Public roads, you ride for free.

CONTACT NUMBERS
The Midlands Meander Association:
(033) 330-8195
info@midlandsmeander.co.za
www.midlandsmeander.co.za
Map info: Craig Beech at cbeech@mighty.co.za

BEWARE OF
Dangerous drivers. Keep to your side of the road when cornering on fast downhills.

THUMBS DOWN
It would be great if the mountain bike touring routes of this scenic area were identified, mapped and seriously marketed.

BEST RIDING REGION

Province: Western Cape **Closest Town:** Swellendam **Distance:** 10–58km

Country roads, stock footpaths, 4x4 routes, swooping forest singletrack – you'll get it all...

OVERBERG

Swellendam, the third oldest magisterial district in South Africa, nestles in the foothills of the spectacular Langeberg range approximately two hours from Cape Town along the N2 highway. Set centrally within the Overberg region of the Western Cape, these magnificent mountains stretch parallel to the Indian Ocean from the Hex River Valley near Worcester in the west to beyond the small farming village of Riversdale in the east.

Descend from the foothills of the Langeberg and adjacent Sonderend Mountains into the fertile valley of the Breede and onto the undulating coastal plains beyond, and you will discover a multitude of nature reserves, private conservancies and wilderness areas as well as the Bontebok National Park.

Few regions in South Africa offer such a variety of diverse riding options as the valleys, slopes and mountains gracing this magnificent mix of mountain plantations, farmland valleys, grassland plateaus and fynbos slopes. The rides in the region are diverse, serving up anything from a jolting and flat crank through the Bontebok National Park, a mountainous jeep and singletrack cruise through Marloth and a challenging, multi-terrain trail that runs through the Grootvadersbosch Conservancy. With the exception of the Bontebok National Park, most of the rides tend to be moderately steep.

PREVIOUS PAGE: The Grootvadersbosch landscape unfolds from a viewpoint above the forest station. LEFT: Dune and beach riding near Arniston present endless opportunities for exploring this unspoilt coastline.

60%

DISTANCE – A challenging 10–58km circular ride

70%

TIME IN THE SADDLE – 5–8 hours

70%

DANGER – Steep inclines, loss of traction, river crossings, mud

60%

TECHNICAL LEVEL – Obstacles include overgrown trails, gravelly surfaces, eroded tracks

70%

GRADIENT – Steep mountain routes, climbs and descents

65%

DIFFICULTY RATING – Difficult

Rated by Jacques Marais

The setting

Stretching from the sandy coastal plains of the Cape south coast to the serrated Cape Fold peaks of the Langeberg, the Overberg region encompasses a rich and diverse range of ecosystems. A picturesque national park where herds of bontebok, red hartebeest and Cape mountain zebra graze upon coastal Renosterveld plains. Grand mountainscapes blanketed in fragrant pine plantations, ramrod stands of soaring sequoia redwoods and breathtakingly beautiful indigenous montane forests. A languid and lazy river meandering through wheatfields. Fynbos patchworks dotted with friendly rural towns. Relic remnants of indigenous montane forest and expansive softwood plantations are juxtaposed with marine estuaries, freshwater marshes, coastal Renosterveld scrub and Cape mountain fynbos against some of the higherlying slopes.

The selection of conservation destinations in the region boggles the mind. There is the 37 000-hectare De Hoop Nature Reserve that preserves freshwater vleis, a diverse inter-tidal zone and one of the largest remaining expanses of indigenous lowland and coastal fynbos. Or Grootvadersbosch Nature Reserve (incorporating the adjacent conservancy and Boosmansbos Wilderness Area) that protects the Cape's most remarkable remaining indigenous forest. Marloth Nature Reserve boasts tea-coloured mountain creeks, plunging waterfalls and swooping singletrack traversing a pristine mountain catchment area. The Riviersonderend Conservation area encompasses a 70 000-hectare haven where farmland and dense riverine vegetation spill over onto a mix of fynbos and forested slopes. Salmonsdam Nature Reserve offers a superb mix of forest, secret gorges and fynbos ridges, while the Bontebok National Park allows you to cruise a little piece of Renosterveld paradise enfolded by the lazy sweep of the Breede River. And last, but certainly not least, there is the incomparable Kogelberg Biosphere Reserve, arguably the most diverse and beautiful botanical 'hot spot' anywhere on our lonely blue planet.

Besides the magnificent trees, the rich diversity of fauna in the area will continue to delight mountain bikers. Leopard, bushbuck, grey rhebuck, sugarbirds, black harriers and numerous species of reptiles, amphibians and insects inhabit the varied biomes, augmenting the incredible range of attractions that awaits you in the Overberg.

ABOVE: Crossing the river near the Grootvadersbosch homestead will come as a welcome relief after a punishing ride along mountainous terrain.

How to get there

Swellendam is centrally situated within the Overberg and offers a perfect springboard into the various eco-destinations and towns of the region. This tree-filled and historic town dates back to 1743 and stretches along the N2 highway, exactly 220km from Cape Town on the way to George.

You will find the turn-off to Grootvadersbosch Nature Reserve between Swellendam and Heidelberg, along the R324. The reserve's entrance is located 12km from where the tarmac road becomes gravel.

Best rides

This was always going to be a tough choice (which explains the reasoning behind the selection of the Overberg as 'Best Riding Region'). Route options are varied, with coastal cruises, challenging forest rides, plantation singletrack, national park rambles, gravel road meanders and hardcore mountain routes all clamouring for attention. The selection of the top three trails below attempts to cover the various levels of riding options available, but there are a great many other rides as well.

Grootvadersbosch

If you're up for a challenging ride, the Grootvadersbosch Conservancy Cycle Trail traverses a rollicking, in-your-face route through conservancy farmland and the adjacent Grootvadersbosch Nature Reserve. Vegetation along the route varies from dense montane forest and mountain fynbos to lowland Renosterveld and rural farmland unfolding along the undulating Langeberg range. Note that group sizes are limited to 12 riders, with a maximum of 24 bikes on the trail at any one time. The 58km route is marketed as a two-day trail with possible stopovers at a variety of accommodation establishments set within the conservancy.

We suggest going high and hectic, cranking into the suck of gravity along the looming Langeberg range. Drop down from the camp site to the Duiwenhoks River, then grind up a steep forestry road on the opposite side of the valley, keeping right at three forks in the road. (Although the route is reasonably well marked, some of the wooden route markers are low on the ground and difficult to spot amongst the thick underbrush.) At the third fork right (2km), you will carve down a looping fynbos barrel before ascending onto a jarring, high plateau ride for a further 3km. Turn right at 5.5km, contouring along the Langeberg foothills in a

HOW TO RIDE OVER ROOTS AND LOGS

1) **Root cause** – tree roots pose a formidable obstacle and you should approach them at a right angle to avoid having your front wheel deflected to square up and pitch you over the handlebars.

2) **Dip down** – force your front suspension down sharply just before hitting a root in order to 'pop' your front wheel over the offending root.

3) **Bottoms up** – move your weight forward on the bike as soon as your front wheel has cleared the root, thus allowing the back wheel to pass effortlessly over the root.

4) **Log jam** – use a similar technique, again approaching the log at ninety degrees, lifting and lunging your front wheel before using the chain ring to get the frame across.

5) **Stump jumping** – if you have sufficient momentum, go the 'bunny hop' route. Kick down in the pedals and lift the bike into the air, bending your legs to help the wheels clear logs.

RIGHT: Marloth Nature Reserve near Swellendam offers a rollicking ride along the Langeberg slopes.

westerly direction to meander along a fairly challenging section of jeep track consisting mainly of coarse sandstone stretches, bush-cutter trails and patches of sand. Around the 8km mark, road quality deteriorates even further as the track bears south and you negotiate a series of deeply dippy drops into rocky mountain streams where perilous water crossings lie in wait for your front wheel.

If you find this trying, wait until you hit the rock chute blasting down towards Grootvadersbosch Farm. At the 11km mark, pass through a gate and into the angry and eroded gravel coils sideswiping along the precipitous slope into the valley below. Take extreme care along this section, as the lack of traction and hazardous terrain will test your downhill riding skills to the max. A few hundred metres before the bottom, there is another gate leading onto the river and a stretch of lush green irrigation fields surrounding the old Grootvadersbosch homestead (13km). Various choices await you here: either turn left just before the homestead and follow the trail back into the forest via Snelsetter or the Honeywood Guest Cottages, or turn left at 13.8km onto the main gravel access road towards Grootvadersbosch. (To do the full 58km route, cross this road and continue southward along the Farmland Trail section.)

If you ride back along the gravel road, you will get straight into a steep climb. Otherwise the off-road route follows an old jeep and singletrack section and will make for far more interesting riding than the slightly mindless slog along the gravel road back to the reserve office.

Follow the signs to Grootvadersbosch, keeping left at forks in the road at 17km, 19km and 20km before dropping down past the turn-off to the lovely Honeywood Guest Farm. A nasty little climb delivers a last sting in the tail before you wheel into the jade embrace of Grootvadersbosch camp site for a well-deserved break.

Bontebok National Park

The Bontebok National Park is situated to the south of the N2 from Swellendam and offers a more relaxing off-road option. It is an easy cruise from town, crossing the N2 and descending along a dirt road with a reasonable surface (watch out for loose gravel patches and the odd pothole, though). Obtain a permit (which includes an adequate map that indicates the network of dirt roads through the park) at the entrance gate, which is situated approximately 8km from the centre of town.

The Bontebok National Park protects a large section of coastal Renosterveld, offering sanctuary to 11 species of frog, 17 species of reptile and more than 200 species of birds, as well as mammals such as the endangered bontebok, Cape mountain zebra, red hartebeest, clawless otter, aardwolf and caracal.

Wind it up along a fast and pockmarked downhill that descends towards the Breede River, keeping right at the 2km mark to follow the longer, right-hand loop zooming towards the camp site on the river's edge (13km). Break here for a dip in the tranquil pools to cool off, then saddle up and take on the jarring right-hand loop climbing back up towards the Langeberg in an anti-clockwise direction. Road surface along this section is scattered with gravel and small rocks, thus turning the 15km return to the gate into a moderately hard ride. There is an easier option – take a short cut straight back past the Old Race Course for a quick 6km cruise to the gate.

Facilities include chalet or caravan accommodation and camping in a serene spot overlooking the slow flow of the Breede, the perfect base from which to indulge in nature trails, swimming, angling, game viewing or just sitting on a rock and watching the sunset.

More mountain bike trails are in the pipeline, so check with the office for all available options. (028) 514-2735

Kogelberg Biosphere Reserve

If you have been searching for the proverbial 'heart of the Cape floral kingdom', look no further. This landscape of steep kloofs, forests, pristine mountain rivers and marine estuaries contain more than 1 600 plant species, of which at least 150 are endemic to the 18 000-hectare core section of the actual Kogelberg Nature Reserve. Peregrine falcons, fish eagles, micro-frogs, endemic freshwater crabs, dainty grysbok and Cape clawless otter roam within the untouched spaces of this remote fynbos wilderness, adding to the diversity of this very fragile sanctuary.

Two mountain biking options are possible: the first is a shortish return ride along the Palmiet River Valley and the second is a longer, one-way ride from near Grabouw along the whole length of the reserve. The **Palmiet River Valley MTB Trail** starts from the Oudebosch office along a short section of singletrack before you turn right past the

OPPOSITE: When you're not cycling, give the gut-thumping flying fox slide into the Buffelsjag Dam a try.

manager's house and then left onto a steep, two-spoor jeep track following the river course in a northwesterly direction. Scenic views across the peaceful Palmiet are breathtaking and more than make up for the moderate climbs ascending into the higher reaches of the reserve. After approximately 5km, the track crosses a concrete causeway before climbing sharply and bearing right; ignore the two roads to your left here and continue onwards through stretches of sand and up a few more rocky climbs. After nearly 13km, you will reach Stokoei Bridge, the turn-around point where a Pepsi-coloured pool is sure to lure you into the river's cool embrace.

The **Kogelberg MTB Trail**, although downhill for much of the route, offers a supreme challenge to endurance riders. Not only will you need to plan a pick-up at the end of the ride, but the 40km route may take up to four hours or more to complete in terrain that some riders may find very challenging. Pedal from Mispah Youth Camp alongside the Kogelberg Dam, turning right after 800m at the route marker (a small wooden sign of an apple). It is important to get a map, as the route follows bush tracks through private property, across rivers on a pulley system and then onto a mowed route known as 'Fynbos Lane'.

A general rule of thumb is to stick close to the power lines up to where the route crosses the Palmiet River at the Halfway Hut (19km). A section of rough track along extremely eroded terrain then traces the southeastern side of the river for a while until it crosses back over the blackwater stream at Stokoei Bridge (26km). From here, you follow the same down-ride as the Palmiet River Valley MTB Trail, making your way down to the Oudebosch office (39km).

Negotiations with the private land owners are ongoing, so please check with the office before you go whether the trail is open. (028) 271-5138

When to go

The Langeberg lies along a transitional zone between summer and winter rainfall areas and precipitation may therefore be expected at any time of the year. May to July is generally the driest time of the year and temperatures may drop as low as 2°C, while the summer highs may reach a red-hot 40°C or more. The period from December to March goes hand in hand with both the highest rainfall and daytime temperature, so opt for shady rides at this time of year.

Kogelberg may be influenced by its proximity to the Indian Ocean, but its climate is still fairly typical of the Western Cape, so expect the winters to be wet.

Off-the-bike entertainment

The Overberg region is filled with a superb array of both indoor and outdoor attractions. Trip back in time on a walk through the Zuurbraak mission village or at the Old Drostdy in Swellendam, a complex that features tourist shops, restaurants and a museum dating back to 1747.

A great many weavers, artists and crafters have relocated to the abundant surroundings of the Overberg area and the region has become famous for the high quality and beauty of the pottery, food, woodcraft, paintings and traditional articles that are on offer here.

Most of the action, however, will be taking place in what amounts to a veritable outdoor Superbowl. In addition to the magnificent mountain bike trails, you have the option of horse riding in Marloth Nature Reserve, game viewing in the Bontebok National Park or rafting the relatively safe rapids of the Breede River.

The six-day Swellendam Trail poses a formidable challenge to hikers, while countless day hikes and trails will seduce walkers in search of a quick, fresh air fix.

Imposing kloofs, whitewater kayaking, adrenalin-inducing zip-wire rocketing into the Buffeljags Dam, sunset booze cruises, bird watching, youngberry liqueur tasting, renowned wine estates, fly- and saltwater fishing, the Malgas Pont ferry, secluded beaches, a fairy sanctuary, whale watching. The only limitation to what you do in the Overberg will be the amount of time you have on your hands.

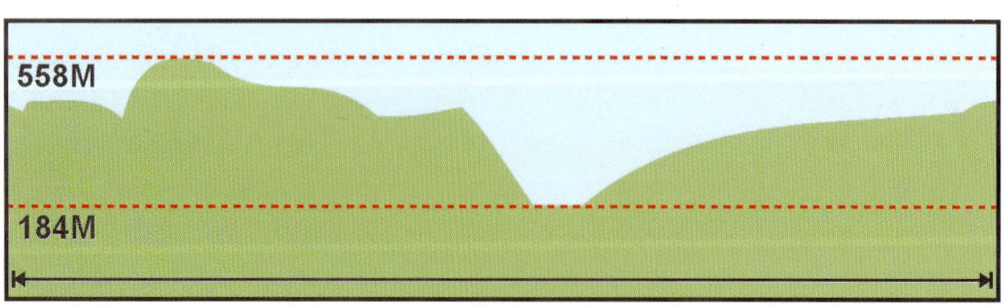

OPPOSITE: Sequoia redwoods tower skywards in the Grootvadersbosch Nature Reserve near Heidelberg. LEFT: The main section of the ride – returning along the gravel road. To do the full 58km route, continue southward along the Farmland Trail section.

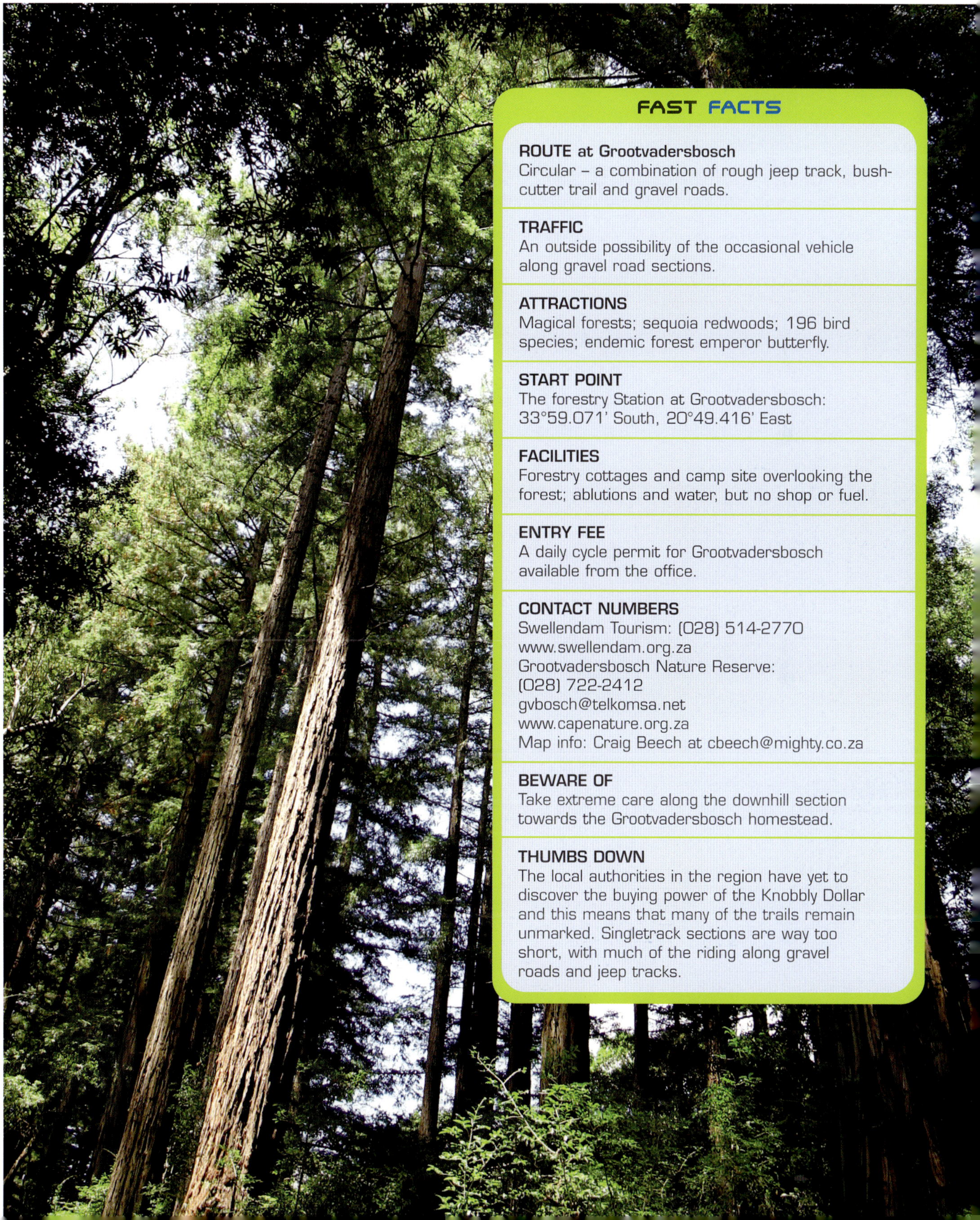

FAST FACTS

ROUTE at Grootvadersbosch
Circular – a combination of rough jeep track, bush-cutter trail and gravel roads.

TRAFFIC
An outside possibility of the occasional vehicle along gravel road sections.

ATTRACTIONS
Magical forests; sequoia redwoods; 196 bird species; endemic forest emperor butterfly.

START POINT
The forestry Station at Grootvadersbosch: 33°59.071' South, 20°49.416' East

FACILITIES
Forestry cottages and camp site overlooking the forest; ablutions and water, but no shop or fuel.

ENTRY FEE
A daily cycle permit for Grootvadersbosch available from the office.

CONTACT NUMBERS
Swellendam Tourism: (028) 514-2770
www.swellendam.org.za
Grootvadersbosch Nature Reserve:
(028) 722-2412
gvbosch@telkomsa.net
www.capenature.org.za
Map info: Craig Beech at cbeech@mighty.co.za

BEWARE OF
Take extreme care along the downhill section towards the Grootvadersbosch homestead.

THUMBS DOWN
The local authorities in the region have yet to discover the buying power of the Knobbly Dollar and this means that many of the trails remain unmarked. Singletrack sections are way too short, with much of the riding along gravel roads and jeep tracks.

BIGGEST LUNG-BUSTER

Province: Eastern Cape **Closest Towns:** Rhodes/Barkly East **Distance:** 84km

A legendary 22km climb, generous lashings of natural grandeur, a deathwish downhill chicane… what more could you ask for?

RHODES

Dominated by the majestic buttresses and spurs of the southern ranges of the Drakensberg, the Victorian era village of Rhodes, and its adjacent neighbours, Lady Grey, Barkly East, Maclear and Elliot, languish within a stretch of prime sheep-farming country where diamond smugglers, cattle rustlers and gamblers once ruled supreme.

Nestled as it is amongst the foothills of the plateau rising up towards the high Lesotho mountains, Rhodes lies a considerable distance from major urban centres. Visitors who commit to the gravel road trek, though, will soon be charmed by the laid-back rural lifestyle. High tea at the Rhodes Hotel (or an *opskop* in the pub), negotiating the high road over Naudé's Nek (at 2 621m the highest pass in the country) or simply relaxing in the magnificent mountains are just a few ways of passing the perfect day.

The mountain biking will not be remotely relaxing though, despite the fact that the riding will generally be along good gravel surfaces. Understand this – you are in mountain goat country and you can expect to be on excellent terms with your granny gear if you plan to pedal the high country around Rhodes.

PREVIOUS PAGE: Green hills and meandering country roads epitomise the serene rural surrounds of Rhodes.
LEFT: Endless panoramas and infinite space make mountain biking in the Drakensberg an unforgettable experience.

80%

DISTANCE – A mean-spirited 84km

70%

TIME IN THE SADDLE – 5–7 hours

80%

DANGER – Hectic concrete downhill, loss of traction during and after rain; subzero temperatures

70%

TECHNICAL LEVEL – Around 30km of the route is good; the rest occupies the space between bad and ugly

100%

GRADIENT – Maximum points as far as climbing is concerned

80%

DIFFICULTY RATING – Difficult

Rated by Jacques Marais

The setting

Impressive peaks surround you wherever you look, with the towering Ben MacDhui (3 001m) and Bonnyvale Peak (2 633m) standing especially tall. July to August in the southern Berg is characterised by heavy snowfalls and this, together with tumbling waterfalls, glinting icicles and waving fields of alpine and subalpine grasses, makes for a fairytale winter landscape. At the base of the slopes, clear mountain creeks meander amongst weeping willows and tall reeds, feeding pools filled with the silvery flash of wild trout out on the prowl. Nearly 200 bird species have been recorded within this predominantly mountain grassland habitat, with regular sightings of flagship species such as black eagle, bearded vulture, southern crowned crane and blue korhaan. The coming of spring is heralded by luminous days and fields of delicate flowers, the latter perfuming the air with their fresh fragrance and splashing the jade hills in a sublime range of muted colours.

The true attraction of the region would have to be the spectacularly stratified rock formations that shape the primordial peaks, abrupt cliffs and prehistoric caves where Bushman hunter-gatherers sheltered in centuries gone by.

How to get there

Rhodes may be accessed either off the N6 or the N2, but youll have to commit to driving on some gravel road in both cases. If you are travelling south along the N6, turn left towards Lady Grey at Aliwal North and follow the R58 to Barkly East (128km). From here, turn left along a good gravel road (the R396) to Moshesh's Ford (34km) and on to Rhodes (about another 30km). Although Aliwal North is less than 200km away, you should expect to spend at least three hours behind the wheel.

The ride

If the weather gods are smiling upon you, it will be a cool and clear day as you set off along the gently undulating road meandering from the sleepy village (1 810m). Don't be lulled into a false sense of security though – after a moderate 10km warm-up ascent, all kinds of mind and body alarms will kick in as you hit the lower reaches of Naudé's Nek, undoubtedly the meanest mother of all mountain passes.

OPPOSITE: Once you've made it to the top of Naudé's Nek, 99% of all other South African gravel climbs will pale into insignificance.

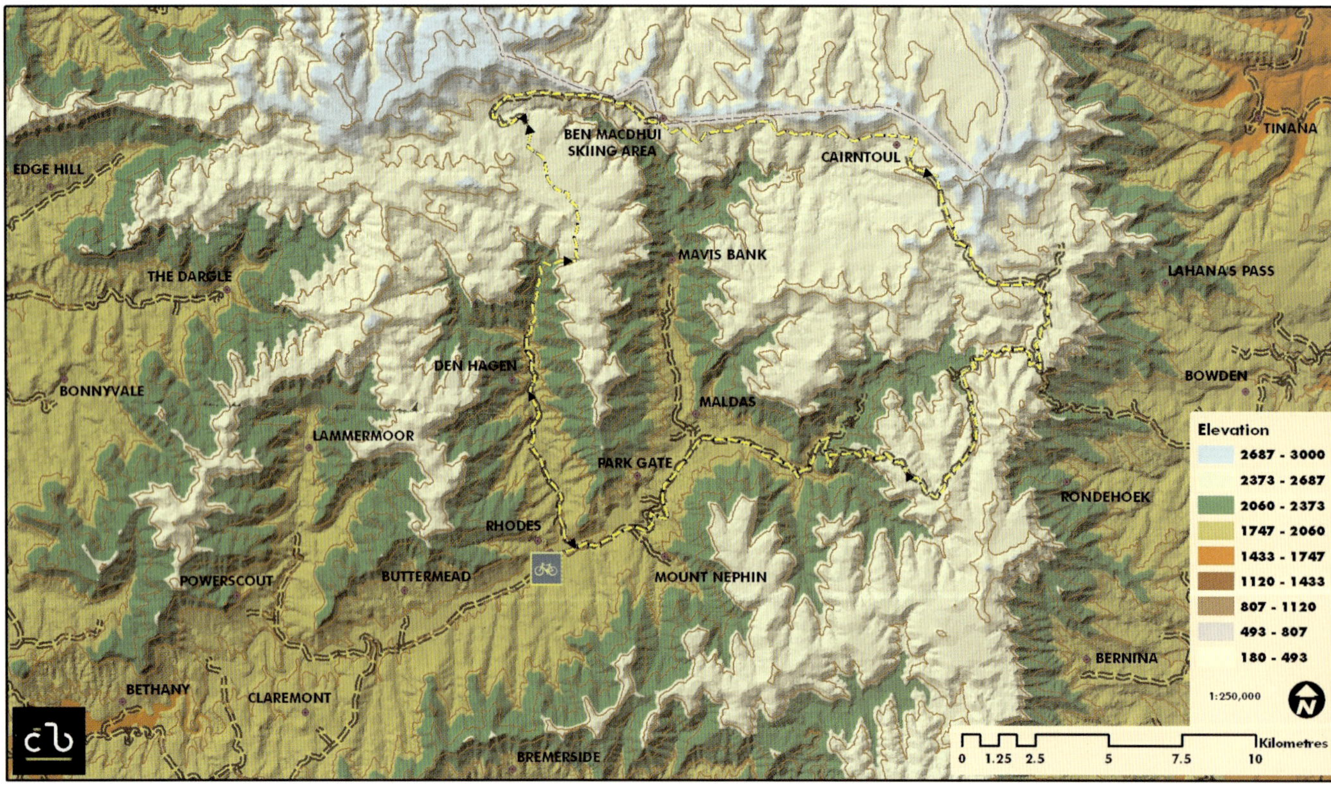

HOW TO SURVIVE A MEAN DOWNHILL

1) **Max headroom** – wear a helmet; if you don't, you deserve to crack your skull open. Also make sure that your helmet has been tested to comply with international safety ratings and that it fits well.

2) **Brake stakes** – check your brakes before you set off on the ride to make sure they are in good working order. Apply braking pressure gently, equalizing the friction between both the rear and the front wheels.

3) **Butt back** – move your body back off the bike so that your stomach is positioned above the saddle, thus avoiding compressing the front shocks and going over the handlebars.

4) **Fatal traction** – keep your wheels in contact with the road surface if you're not confident of your bike skills. This is no time to try out a trick for the first time.

5) **Speed limit** – ride according to your own ability. Along a steep downhill, it is easy to get carried away on a wave of adrenalin. Play it safe and you will live to ride it faster the next time around.

Spinning is the name of the game, so gear down and get the cadence going as you grind through curve upon switchback upon S-bend upon more curves on your way to the mythical summit that awaits you after a resolute, unfailing 22km ascent. (There is one flailing downhill run at the 22km mark, but this is just to mess with your head, so it's perfectly acceptable for you to cry or, if you prefer, to pray to the deity of your choice. Whatever you do, don't turn back because it will all be worthwhile in the end.)

At the Naudé's Nek apex (2 621m), turn north off the main road (32km) to follow a rocky track along the escarpment towards the Cairntoul police stock theft unit before bearing west.

Do not be deluded by a few slips of downhill along the way – all too soon you'll be cranking into the teeth of gravity en route to Lesotho's View (52km), that is the highest point along your ride at 2 732m.

Dead legs, hallucinations of ice-cold beers and panoramic vistas across Lesotho will keep you company as you buck and jolt along tracks of the MacDhui Flats on your approach to Tiffindell. Bear left here, following the road away from the ski resort as the downhill begins to flex its gradient. Feather your brakes a few times as you approach the 70km mark, for you are about to start the hairiest downhill of your life.

This is the infamous Carlisle's Hoek Pass, where everything suddenly goes into free-fall mode. Over the next 3km, you will descend more than 300m, sometimes at a gradient in excess of 1:3.

Traction along the dual concrete strip road may be extremely sketchy in wet weather and these helter-skelter hairpins have been responsible for more broken bones than you would care to know about, so please keep your cool. Beyond this white-knuckle zone, the route levels out gradually and bombs into the valley along a relatively moderate decline for 5km. Holler 'Yeeha!' at the top of your lungs as you cross the Bell River and cruise back into the village. You have just done more than eighty hardcore kilometres in the saddle.

When to go

A visit to Rhodes goes hand in hand with constantly changing weather, so ready yourself for the four seasons in a single day scenario. A glorious summer day may switch at the drop of a helmet to a scary electrical storm complete with pelting hailstones and lightning, while the winter months bring rain, sleet, fog and substantial snowfalls. Summer evenings are generally cool and peaceful though, while spring and autumn make for brisk cycling weather.

Other rides

The Rhodes MTB Challenge route is but the tip of the iceberg as far as off-road riding goes in the Rhodes region. A multitude of farm road meanders, and steep 4x4 tracks linked to a range of farm stays in the area beg exploration, while the surrounding towns of Maclear, Barkly East and Ugie also offer lots of opportunities for a mountain bike ride.

Approximately halfway between Rhodes and Barkly East along the R396, a sign to Bokspruit will set you down

OPPOSITE: Although much of the riding is along jeep track, the surface may be challenging in places.

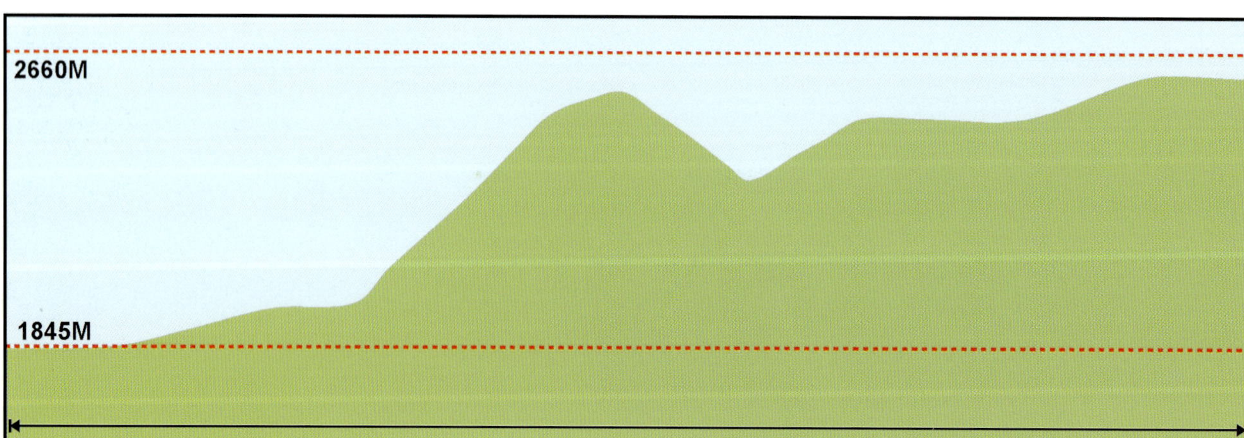

Warning: This profile is an approximation.

on a gravel road into an untouched little piece of paradise filled with frolicking waterfalls and cascading creeks.

A reasonably flat, 40km-plus return ride along the road from **Gateshead Cottage** (a sublime country hideaway if you want to hike, fly-fish and mountain bike to your heart's content) offers a leisurely gravel cruise. Rock-hopping and sheep-track riding options also abound along the edge of the spruit, allowing you to up the excitement levels.

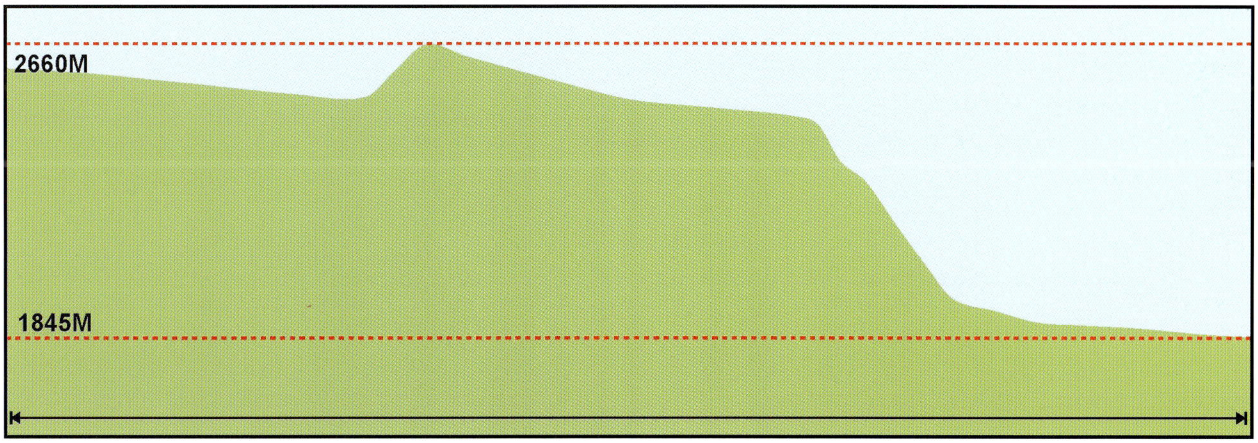

A multi-day ride traversing private farms in the Bokspruit area is also an option, where a gnarly crossing of the Bulhoek Pass makes up part of the ride.

Closer to Maclear, more off-road riding may be had on **Hope Holiday Farms**. Again, most of the riding is along farm roads, but the many cattle tracks and walking trails along the Mooi River are sure to entice riders not averse to a bit of portaging. Affordable accommodation in rondavels, with stunning views across the densely wooded river course and undulating Drakensberg foothills, makes this a truly awesome outdoor adventure stopover.

If you're based at **Tiffindell**, bang yourself down onto a raw and rude downhill run skittering along the Wartrail Road. The first 10km of riding along the grassy plateau is relatively flat, but the gradient goes ballistic as soon as you pop your front wheel onto the first gravel switchback to plunge headlong over the escarpment. Twenty nine kilometres and an almost 1 000m difference in height later, you will bottom out on a heart-thumping high, ready to take on the three-hour return ride, or maybe not! Promise we won't tell if you get your buddies to come and pick you up.

Off-the-bike entertainment

A visit to the picturesque village of Rhodes in the northern reaches of the mountainous Eastern Cape will allow you to experience the charm of a forgotten era.

Don't miss the Bell's Whisky Wild Trout Fly-fishing Festival in March, an annual quad bike and off-road Moto-X Rally in February, or the winter snow sport season at Tiffindell Ski Resort (where you can down schnapps while strapped by your ankles to the ceiling of the highest pub in South Africa). (011) 787-9090

The Ben MacDhui Trail, a 51km/three-day circular hike from Rhodes, will not only keep you out of the saddle for a few days, but will also set you down on the summit of Ben MacDhui, at 3 001m the highest peak in what used to be the old Cape Province.

Nearby Maclear offers an easier walk where you can view fossilised dinosaur footprints believed to be more than 200 million years old.

Contact the Rhodes Hotel to find out more about options such as horse trails, wing shooting, challenging 4x4 routes, kloofing, climbing, scrambling and country drives. (045) 974-9308

NEXT PAGE: The picturesque village of Rhodes nestling within the Drakensberg foothills.

FAST FACTS

ROUTE
A circular gravel route sky-lining from Rhodes along 38km of good gravel road and 46km of gnarly dirt.

TRAFFIC
Maybe a few vehicles along Naudé's Nek, but chances are that it will be just you and your bike on this ride.

ATTRACTIONS
Majestic mountain views; great gulps of fresh air; rare bird sightings; winter wonderland; trout streams.

START POINT
Rhodes Village:
30°47.745' South, 27°57.947' East

FACILITIES
Rhodes Hotel, Walkerbouts Inn, plus a range of B&Bs and farm stays abound.

ENTRY FEE
Public roads, so you ride for free.
Access to private land should be easy to arrange.

CONTACT NUMBERS
Ukhahlamba Region Tourism: (045) 974-9900
tour-escape@telkomsa.net
Rhodes Tourism Office: (045) 974-9290
dave@wildtrout.co.za
Walkerbouts Inn: (045) 974-9290
Map info: Craig Beech at cbeech@mighty.co.za

BEWARE OF
Weather prone to rapid change; extremely steep downhill along Carlisle's Hoek; slippery terrain when wet.

THUMBS DOWN
Despite the incredible beauty of the area, this is very much a ride along a (very gnarly in places) dirt road. Plus, getting to Rhodes from anywhere in South Africa will mean spending quite a few hours cooped up in a car.

HOTTEST RIDE

Province: Northern Cape **Closest Towns:** Sendelingsdrift/Springbok **Total Distance:** 39.8km

...succumb to the stark simplicity of a landscape rampant with runaway mountain ranges, shifting seas of sand, bizarre forests of 'half-mens' trees and nomadic Nama shepherds...

RICHTERSVELD

Situated within the extreme northwest corner of South Africa, hunkered down within the muddy embrace of the mighty Gariep, you will find the expansive 160 000-hectare Richtersveld National Park. This mountain desert reserve offers a complete escape from everything urban. Facilities are limited to low, brick fireplaces and a few bristly desert trees (and are in some cases non-existent), although park authorities are currently in the process of upgrading some of the camp sites by adding basic ablution facilities. So don't expect any luxuries when you arrive, clouded in red dust and good karma, at one of the five designated camping spots – De Hoop, Pootjiespram and Richtersberg on the river, with De Koei and Kokerboomkloof inland.

Self-sufficiency is a must if you're headed into this minimalist tableau of rock, sand and succulents, so ensure you have enough water, fuel and supplies to cope with any unforeseen emergencies. A sturdy 4x4 is required to negotiate some of the burlier routes, but a two-wheel drive vehicle with reasonable ground clearance will cope with many of the park roads. Opt for a river stay if it's your first visit – the proximity of the water takes the edge off the searing heat, dust and lack of shelter. Once you've settled in, hike to your heart's content, drift down the gentle rapids on an inflatable tube, indulge in a spot of fly-fishing or climb the razorback peaks crowding in close to the river.

The mountain biking will be challenging, especially along the many sandy sections, and it will certainly be a test of both character and endurance.

PREVIOUS PAGE: Halfmens and kokerboom trees stand guard over a lunar expanse near Richtersberg.
LEFT: A cycling expedition in the Richtersveld should preferably be undertaken with a backup vehicle.

40%

DISTANCE – A moderate 39.8km return/circular ride

40%

TIME IN THE SADDLE – 3–4 hours

90%

DANGER – Exposure, dust storms, thorns, venomous snakes, scorpions and spiders

90%

TECHNICAL LEVEL – Extreme corrugations, deep sand, pebble fields, thorns, rutted tracks, lack of traction

50%

GRADIENT – A gentle ascent plus a few short, sharp climbs

60%

DIFFICULTY RATING – Difficult

Rated by Jacques Marais

The setting

Once your headspace adjusts to the vast stretch of the ochre alluvial plains, jutting volcanic rock and the ferocious onslaught of the elements, the allure of the Richtersveld will surreptitiously begin to weave its spell. Contorted, smelly shepherd's trees (*Boscia albitrunca*), the alien loom of euphorbias, the antics of barking geckos – all will slowly but surely get under your skin. And when a gazillion glimmering stars swoon against the velvet black of the night, seemingly close enough for you to raise your hand and pluck one from the sky, you will grasp the desert's fatal attraction.

The harsh landscape, which consists in certain places of lava, porphyry and tuff more than 2 000 million years old, is a place of a myriad moods.

Baster kokerboom, shepherd's tree and Karoo boerbean offer low cover along sandy riverbeds, while the lush vegetation along the river coils through the arid ranges like the fecund trail of a giant green python. Mammals are scarce, but you are sure to bump into your fair share of reptiles and arthropods (beetles, scorpions and spiders). Keep an eye out for the *Parabuthus granulatus*, an exceptionally large and mean-spirited nocturnal scorpion, and probably the most poisonous of its kind in southern Africa. Birds abound along the river's edge, and sightings of fish eagles, darters, warblers, swifts and kingfishers will be on the cards.

OPPOSITE: Craggy rockscapes dwarf riders wearing protective shirts to shield them from the fierce sun.
LEFT: You may encounter Damara fat-tailed sheep and their nomadic herders in the Richtersveld.

How to get there

The main access route to the Richtersveld is along the N7 passing through Springbok and onward to Steinkopf (52km), where you turn left along the R382 to Port Nolloth (93km). A gravel road turning right towards Lekkersing offers a rather long short cut, so I would advise you stick to the tar. The next town is Alexander Bay (85km), where you turn right towards Sendelingsdrift, another 100km along a gravel road (allow 1.5–2 hours). Remember to look out for the park signs as mining in the area is playing havoc with the road network.

Best ride

The sandy gravel roads grinding through this land of wide horizons and stacked rock are sure to remain the domain of endurance mountain bikers for a long time to come. Start off with the moderately difficult ride below and, once you've ascertained your riding ability within the desert environment, start thinking about longer and/or circular route options.

Set off from De Hoop and follow the access road west, pedalling away from the river along a desert track varying from gritty hard-pack and pebble fields to sandy drifts (opt for the more compact sand alongside the road wherever this seems a better option). One or two short, sharp climbs might get your endorphins going, but the overall ascent rates somewhere between gentle and moderate en route to road marker R5 (7.9km). Keep to the right here, meandering

LEFT: Get your butt into gear and climb the peaks above De Hoop for an awesome view along the Gariep.
ABOVE: Relaxing near Kokerboomkloof.

along the foothills of a series of spectacular rock ranges and through eroded gorges until you crank onto the immensity of the Koeroegab Plains, where the road opens up and levels out past marker R4 (another 4.7km). Stop off at the ancient tree just before you reach R4 – to the right of the road a grandfather *boscia* ekes out a tenuous existence, dispatching contorted ground roots to snake across the parched earth.

Keep right again from R4 along a gradual incline towards R3 (4.8km), turning left here towards marker R13 (4.6km) along the road towards Helskloof Gate. Sections of the road between R4 and here are currently under construction and, according to Arid Parks Management, many of these routes will be upgraded over the next few years.

The climb back to R4 (4.3km) is challenging, mainly because of rough road surfaces and sections of energy-sapping sand but, once you hit the return down to De Hoop, you can crank up to the big ring.

As long as you keep up your speed, the cruise back into De Hoop should be a cinch. Chances are you will go over the handlebars at least once, though – we all did at some stage of this ride.

There are two ways in which to approach a Richtersveld cycling experience. The first is to base yourself at one of the camp sites and do daily rides from there, while the second would be to use a support vehicle and circumnavigate the park, cycling to a different camp every night. Your choice, but it makes sense to sleep in one place and avoid having to pitch camp every night after a full day of cycling.

When to go

September to November and April to May are excellent times to get away to the Richtersveld. The hoary winter nights lack some of their severity, the daytime temperatures are not yet at their full intensity and dust storms are less frequent.

Also, once every decade or so, unexpected spring rains might herald an explosion of desert blooms along Koeroegab Plains. Surprisingly, the weather is rather fickle, with mist, winds and cold fronts rolling in from the nearby coast.

Other rides

The route to the Richtersveld is a long and arduous trek, wherever you're coming from, and a relaxing mountain bike stopover along the way will make for a welcome break. Two possible options along the N7 highway stand out, but nothing stops you from doing both...

Goegap Nature Reserve, situated approximately 15km east of Springbok between the N14 and R355, encompasses an area of 15 000 hectares consisting mainly of so-called 'Namaqualand Broken Veldt'. The singular granite koppies and sandy plains of the reserve offer sanctuary to more than 40 mammal and numerous bird species, but the true attraction of the area is the annual floral display for which this region is world-famous.

Biking is along a 4x4 track with some steep riding along Carolusberg, the highest point in the reserve, with distance options of 14 or 20km. Although there is quite a bit of rock and sand, it is possible to adapt the route choice in order to suit your own personal level of fitness. An entrance fee is payable at the gate and an additional rate is levied per rider.

Just on 68km south of Springbok, along the N7, you will find Kamieskroon: arguably one of South Africa's best-kept mountain biking secrets. Four clearly signposted, well-planned routes traverse the Kamiesberg area east of town and will delight greenhorns and gearheads alike.

Nourivier (29km) is a moderate to easy circular route. **Leliefontein A** (8.2km) offers a short ride that is perfect for the whole family while **Leliefontein B** will attract the more accomplished riders. It can be done either as a straight-line 30km (you would need to arrange a pick-up at the end) or a challenging circular route comprising 49km. Finally, there's the easy **Vissersplaat Circular**, a ride of 7.5km offering great scenic views of the area.

Income earned from mountain biking in the area goes to the Leliefontein and Nourivier communities, so you can ride your bike and do a good deed at the same time.

Off-the-bike entertainment

If Namaqualand is renowned for one thing only, it is for the area's prolific floral wealth. Every year from August to September, the arid landscape is transformed into a fantastical flower garden filled with a thousand different colours.

Amateur geologists, on the other hand, flock to the Northern Cape to revel in the bountiful mineral treasures of a region where semi-precious stones, crystals and other geological treasures are a dime a dozen.

Rafting trips along the Gariep, South Africa's largest river by far, offer anything from a fun-filled day for the family to a death-defying rapid in the thundering Orange River Gorge.

And, with the Richtersveld nudging right up against Namibia's southern border, it may be an excellent idea to extend your trip long enough to visit the spectacular Fish River Canyon and some of the other outdoor charms offered by our northern neighbour.

OPPOSITE: Death-defying rides along gargantuan granite mounds are sure to get your adrenalin pumping.

HOW TO SURVIVE A DESERT RIDE

1) **Life's a beach** – there will be more sand than at Ballito Bay, so get used to it. Best you read the tips on 'How to Ride in Sand' on page 19 right away.

2) **Extreme exposure** – protect yourself from the sun by wearing breathable, protective clothing and by regularly applying the strongest sunscreen you can lay your hands on.

3) **Siesta time** – the heat will be switched to max from at least 11h00 to 15h00, so plan your riding for the early morning and late afternoons.

4) **Drink and ride** – constant rehydration is necessary to replace the liquids you will be losing due to perspiration. Plan on a minimum of four litres per person per day.

5) **Flat spin** – shale, thorns and various other road hazards will conspire to leave you 'feeling deflated'. Pack spare tubes, a pump and a puncture repair kit.

ABOVE: Fly-fish for wily yellow fish in the gentle rapids near the De Hoop camp site.

OPPOSITE: The vast desert landscape seems to swallow a backup vehicle en route to Richtersberg.

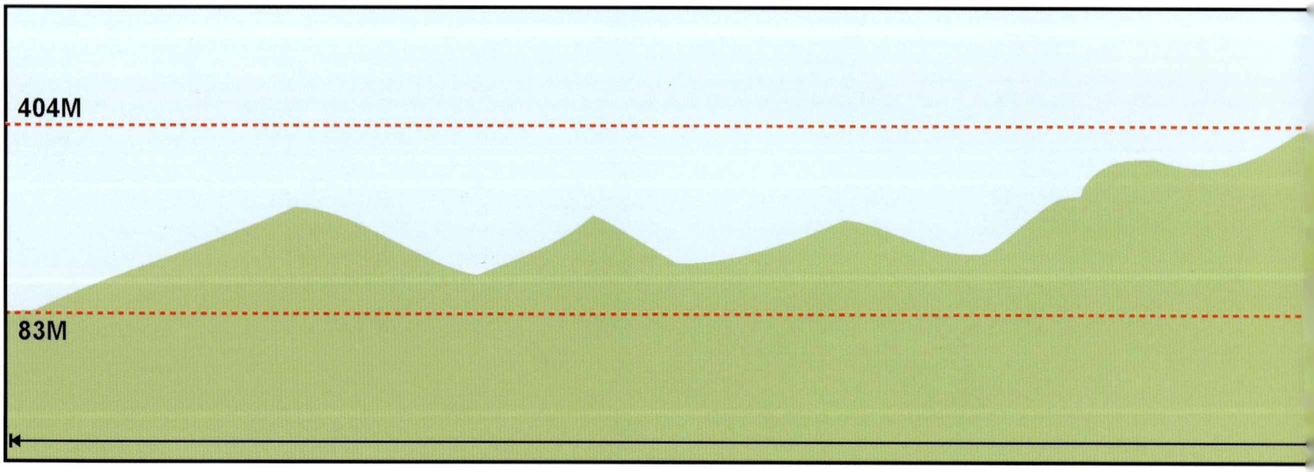

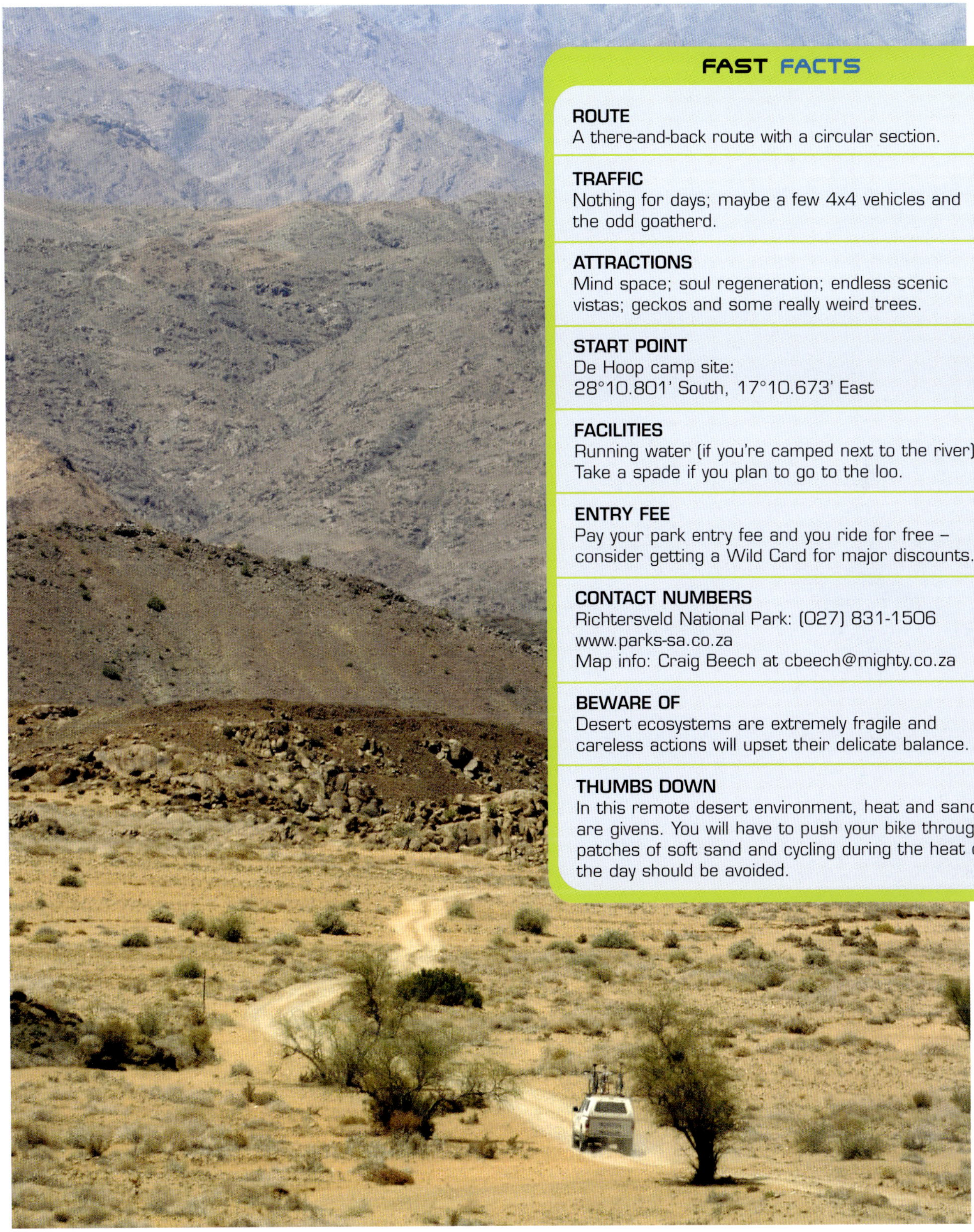

FAST FACTS

ROUTE
A there-and-back route with a circular section.

TRAFFIC
Nothing for days; maybe a few 4x4 vehicles and the odd goatherd.

ATTRACTIONS
Mind space; soul regeneration; endless scenic vistas; geckos and some really weird trees.

START POINT
De Hoop camp site:
28°10.801' South, 17°10.673' East

FACILITIES
Running water (if you're camped next to the river). Take a spade if you plan to go to the loo.

ENTRY FEE
Pay your park entry fee and you ride for free – consider getting a Wild Card for major discounts.

CONTACT NUMBERS
Richtersveld National Park: (027) 831-1506
www.parks-sa.co.za
Map info: Craig Beech at cbeech@mighty.co.za

BEWARE OF
Desert ecosystems are extremely fragile and careless actions will upset their delicate balance.

THUMBS DOWN
In this remote desert environment, heat and sand are givens. You will have to push your bike through patches of soft sand and cycling during the heat of the day should be avoided.

BEST FOREST MECCA

Province: Mpumalanga Closest Town: Sabie Distance: 22km

SABIE

...the sound of your spinning wheels along the tracks is muted by thick deposits of pine needles...

XTC Team

The one venue in Africa capable of hosting a top class world championship mountain bike event would be Sabie. Here you will find purpose-built trails that have resulted from a decade of cross-country racing in one of South Africa's most beautiful settings. Your experience here will ensure you return time and time again.

Apart from the mountain bikers, who feel they have arrived in heaven, tourists have always flocked to Sabie. Strategically placed en route to the Kruger National Park, it is situated within the world's largest man-made forest, an industry established around 1876 to meet the growing demand for gold mining props in South Africa.

In terms of the off-road riding, what you see are the fruits of a small but dedicated group of local off-roadies, namely the Lowveld Chaingang Club and the Mpumalanga MTB Association (MAMBA). These worthy folk have worked closely with major forestry corporates like SAPPI, MONDI, SAFCOL and Global Forestry Products, as well as stakeholders in the local tourism industry, to gain land access for off-road cycling and ensure that it is maintained on the private forestry property surrounding Sabie. Consequently, this has become a prime recreational and racing mecca for mountain biking enthusiasts from all over South Africa.

PREVIOUS PAGE: Get to the start on the Old Lydenburg Road – and grab some post-ride refreshment at a farmstall en route. Once there, take your pick of the forested trails to suit all abilities.
LEFT: The vast majority of Sabie's trails traverse commercial forest – follow the marked routes or explore on your own.

30%

DISTANCE – A short 22km ride

30%

TIME IN THE SADDLE – 2–3 hours

60%

DANGER – Forestry roads on contours. Rain can instantly transform roads into a slippery nightmare

60%

TECHNICAL LEVEL – Loose slate and slippery clay hardpack

50%

GRADIENT – Gradual, but unrelenting

50%

DIFFICULTY RATING – Moderate to difficult *Rated by Herman Mills*

The setting

The vast majority of trails traverse commercial forest, with small pockets of indigenous bush added into the mix. Primates like vervet monkeys and bushbabies can be spotted along watercourses still lined with indigenous jungle growth. Other than this, the vast commercial forests are uncannily silent – with the only sounds being the steady drip of water off the trees, or the whine of sawmills far below and the distant buzzing of chainsaws.

Even the sound of your spinning wheels along some tracks is muted by thick deposits of pine needles and, should you get caught in the mist, the only sound will be you breathing in and out, in and out.

How to get there

From Sabie, get onto the Old Lydenberg Road and follow the signs to the Castle Rock and Merry Pebbles resorts. You can purchase your permit at this resort or at Bike Doc on Main Street in Sabie.

Gather your group together underneath the old railway bridge next to the Castle Rock sign on the road. All mountain bike routes are signposted from here.

Best ride

This 22km ride (the Yellow Trail) starts off from the Castle Rock municipal camp site. A jeep track cruise parallel to the Sabie River, with the tangled growth and moist cliffs of Castle Rock to one side, forms the lovely start of this ride. A singletrack veering to the left quickly lures you off onto some lovingly built, tight singletrack through a tunnel of dense bush and small stands of commercial plantation. This little treat soon reunites you with the jeep track which takes you to the Bridal Veil Falls road, where you turn right and ride along a dirt road for about 1.5km.

Take the left-hand fork that turns off the Falls road, and cycle up the side of the mountain into the Ceylon Forest where you will be introduced to the first of several stiff climbs, guaranteed to make you break out into a sweat. Don't feel too pressurised to ride all this. If you are already suffering, take regular breaks; listen to the trees growing – there are lots more climbs coming!

You will pass over the top of the Bridal Veil Falls, climbing the contours ever higher on little-used forestry roads, where mountain streams drip and trickle and provide convenient places to replenish your water supply or simply splash your

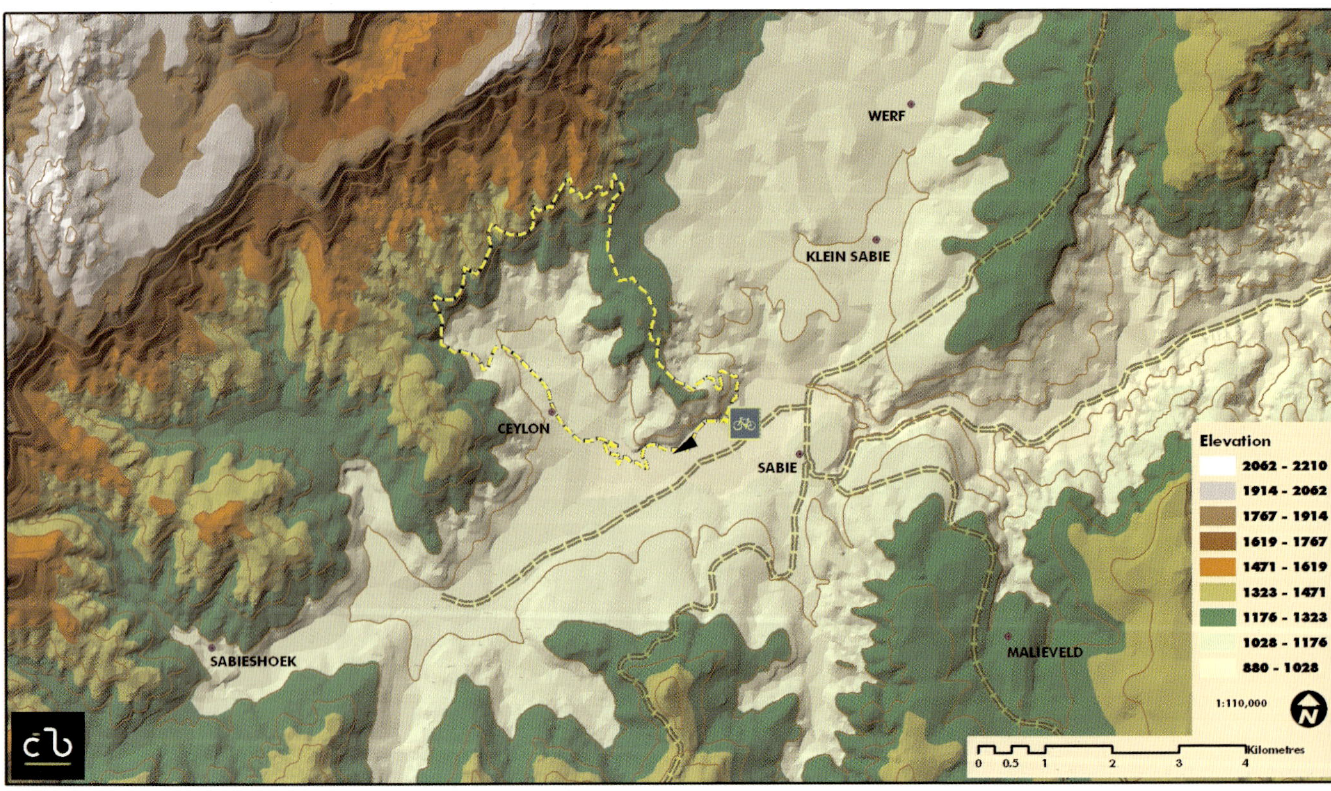

HOW TO AVOID TROUBLE IN THE MOUNTAINS

1) **If weather conditions** are bad – mist, rain, high winds, extreme cold or heat – rather stay at home. They can turn very nasty very quickly up in the mountains.

2) **Let somebody know** which trail you plan to do; and stick to that.

3) **Carry** an all-weather jacket in your pack as well as sufficient water and some energy bars.

4) **Ensure you have** a spare tube or two, and the other common repair items: a pump, tyre levers, chain riveting tool, and a multi-function tool kit. Learn how to use them!

5) **Carry a small light** for your bike in case you are out longer than you anticipated. A small mirror to send a signal is a good idea, and/or a whistle if you get seriously lost and there's a search party out looking for you.

face. Lungs feel supercharged with moisture and oxygen and the smell of pine and eucalyptus, but the clay-like consistency of the soil and constant humidity make the terrain very slick. Loose slate and rocks embedded in the roads add to the slippery mix so you will need to concentrate and keep your speed under control on short downhill sections. On the uphills, expect to spin out on your way to the highest point on the ride (1 400m), which is announced by a fast, rocky road downhill that switchbacks like a mad snake for about 9km. Views are often obscured by the forest, but this can all change when trees are harvested.

You'll see the power lines and come to a T-junction where you go left, and then keep on going right. The route goes through a metamorphosis from good dirt road to rough forestry track within only a few kilometres. Then, quite unexpectedly, you hit some of the most awesome switchback singletrack upon going down the mountain. As you sashay through the trees, riders are strung out ahead and behind like Christmas tree lights. After this piece of cross-country heaven, everyone rolls out smiling onto a forestry road where a short steep downhill will deliver you back to Castle Rock Resort and, too soon, the end of the Yellow Trail.

When to go

Any time of the year. Start very early in the morning. In winter it is cold and dry with high fire risk. In summer the days are humid, hot and wet. Do not leave too late in the afternoon, as it gets dark deceptively early in the forests. Avoid riding in misty conditions.

Other rides

Sabie is the perfect hub for an off-road cycling holiday for anyone, from competitive riders consolidating their training, to families with little fledgling cyclists. There are enough options here for you to do a different ride every day of the week. With the exception of the Yellow and Red trails, all are along forestry roads.

Kids will love the return ride along the first section of the **Yellow Trail**, up to the junction with the Bridal Veil Falls road. Older children will be able to ride to the Falls and back without too much whining. This section of the ride is also suitable for parents with baby trailers or baby chairs.

The Red Trail is 13km and takes about 1–1.5 hours to ride and consists of short steep climbs and technical singletrack through Tweefontein Forest. Singletrack along the river climbs up forestry roads before plunging over the ridge on a series of winding, slithery tracks, a wooden bridge and a 1.5m drop-off down a steep incline to the finish.

The **Blue Trail** is 25km long and it takes 1.5–2 hours of riding. It is a return ride along forestry roads to Maritzbos hiking hut via Lone Creek Falls. There is some easy cruising for the first 8km along the river to Lone Creek, followed by a stiff 2km track up and over the falls that reunites riders with the river and follows the watercourse to the hut. This can be done as either an overnight or a day ride.

ABOVE: Biting bugs like this horsefly will not let you forget that you are in the bush.

The **Green Trail** is 45km and requires between 2.5 and 4.5 hours depending on your fitness level. Follow the Sabie River along trout farms and oak plantations, where an undulating gravel road takes you past Horseshoe Falls. Thereafter, you face a demanding 4km off-road climb up to Misty Mountain Chalets via the Long Tom Pass forestry station.

Views of distant waterfalls and the entire Sabie Valley are food for the soul near the top. Return to town via the tar road, but note that it is by no means downhill all the way either.

The **Black Trail** is suitable for fit, experienced cyclists only. This 45km (that takes 3–5 hours) is a very demanding ride via Maritzbos Forest ascending to above the treeline. Cycle to the Stables hiking hut situated on the slopes of Mount Anderson, the highest peak in Mpumalanga (1 900m).

The pristine flora and fauna, the incredible views and, of course, the 15km downhill back home are the rewards for the long climb. If your brakes are not as good as they should be, your arms and hands will be aching from your deathgrip all the way down. Do this as an overnight or day trail.

The **Umbhaba Lodge MTB Trail** is roughly a 45km ride suitable for intermediate to fit riders. This trail is marked and traverses both the 110-hectare Umbhaba property and some of its neighbouring properties. A mix of indigenous flora and fauna and cash crop plantations will be encountered along the route.

Situated 48km from Sabie on the old R53 between Hazyview and White River, Umbhaba has a restaurant and overnight facilities. Day visitors are most welcome, call them on (013) 737-7636 or visit www.umbhaba.co.za.

Off-the-bike entertainment

Other activities in the area include mile upon mile of quiet, wide tarred roads for exceptional road cycling. There's hiking, horseriding, tubing, river rafting, fly-fishing, and a King Swing in nearby Graskop.

A variety of relaxing day drives can be undertaken from Sabie to nearby small towns like Pilgrim's Rest, Graskop and Hazyview. The Sabie Forestry Museum provides good insight on the history of the area. But best of all, after a hard day of pedalling, Sabie boasts a number of good restaurants for ravenous cyclists.

For more information on the area, call (013) 764-1177 or visit www.sabie.co.za.

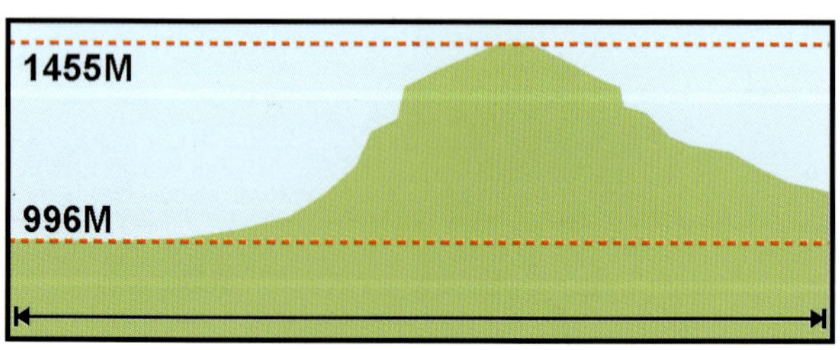

FAST FACTS

ROUTE
A circular 22km route of forestry roads along mountain contours. Optional custom-built mountain bike singletrack of 2km.

TRAFFIC
Shared with hikers and forestry vehicles.

ATTRACTIONS
Commanding views over the escarpment from the highest point and subsequent downhill.

START POINT
Castle Rock Resort:
25°09.372' South, 30°76.944' East

FACILITIES
Ablutions and swimming pool at Castle Rock.

ENTRY FEE
MTB trails all around Sabie are on private property. To ensure continued access, cyclists must purchase a day permit or an overnight pass. Available from Merry Pebbles Resort, off the Old Lydenburg Road, or Bike Doc, Main Street, Sabie.

CONTACT NUMBERS
Merry Pebbles Resort: (013) 764-2266
pebbles@soft.co.za
Bike Doc: (013) 764-1034
bikedoc@lantic.net
Map info: Craig Beech at cbeech@mighty.co.za.

BEWARE OF
Do not ride in the mountains during inclement weather. Fit the correct off-road tyres to your bike. Slicks and semi-slicks are dangerous on the slippery terrain here.

THUMBS DOWN
Trees being harvested can cause downed markers and changing landscape. Trees obscure some of the views on the ride.

OPPOSITE: A welcome pause at the top of a long, hard climb with the rolling resistance of a bed of thick pine needles.

BEST FAMILY-ON-HOLIDAY RIDE

Province: KwaZulu-Natal **Closest Towns:** Umzinto/Scottburgh **Distance:** 20km

SOUTH COAST

...you are guaranteed the most outstanding panoramic views over the Umzinto river valley and the Indian Ocean.

KZN Wildlife has identified areas in some of their parks that are managed according to stringent wilderness principles in an effort to preserve these invaluable natural resources for future generations.

Vernon Crookes Nature Reserve is a good example of a reserve's long-term commitment to ensure that there will always be timeless places where people can freely immerse themselves in a wilderness and be irrevocably changed by it.

Less than one percent of South Africa's land surface is proclaimed wilderness, an indictment on the priorities of modern man where short-term gains lead to long-term losses. It would be unacceptable if our grandchildren were only able to read about the wilds of Africa and what they had been like but were never able to experience it.

So, next time you're on a family holiday on the South Coast of KwaZulu-Natal, take some time out from the beach to experience the magic of this little pocket of wilderness. It is a secure and rare piece of coastal mountain biking paradise.

PREVIOUS PAGE: While the beach is always a tempting option, the Vernon Crookes Reserve offers rides through indigenous coastal forest.
LEFT: Holiday time equals play time.

30%
DISTANCE – A short 20km

30%
TIME IN THE SADDLE – 1–2 hours

60%
DANGER – Fall potential on slippery surfaces

60%
TECHNICAL LEVEL – Tree roots, rough jeep track

50%
GRADIENT – A variety of ascents await you

50%
DIFFICULTY RATING – Moderate to difficult

Rated by Herman Mills

The setting

In what is a most convincing argument in the case for conservation, KwaZulu-Natal's South Coast was historically one of the best known and most popular holiday destinations in South Africa.

The beaches, the warm Indian Ocean and lush rolling green hills became trademarks of this coastline. Today, ugly high-rise buildings cast unwelcome shadows across what once were beautiful beaches, and the coastline is all but stripped of marine life. Inland, much of the indigenous coastal forest has been destroyed to make way for human habitation and cultivation.

But, putting all the environmental disappointments aside, the South Coast is still a marvellous place for a holiday, and pockets of natural beauty can still be found. Probably due to the overwhelming allure of the ocean, few visitors ever consider venturing inland. And it is here that you will find Vernon Crookes Nature Reserve. Anticipating the environmental impact of development along this coastline, the reserve was proclaimed in 1973, and now occupies 2 189 hectares.

Set amongst hills ranging in altitude from 150–610m above sea level, the reserve's most important feature is its beautiful coastal forests. After driving up all those hills into the reserve, you can park your car with complete peace of mind at the main reception, unload and get set. The office staff are engaging and helpful, with a passion for what they do, issuing you with maps and advice to get you going.

You only have a limited area to work with, so a long circular loop is out of the question, but fortunately you can do a series of there-and-back rides that will bring you to the main reception every time.

This is a convenient arrangement for families, or relaxed holidaymakers – some participants of the ride may opt out and let the more energetic in the group do the next section while they relax, play with the children or, better yet, finalise their culinary arrangements in the picnic area that is near the office and dam.

How to get there

Vernon Crookes lies 76.5km from Durban. Take the N2 South and turn off at the Park Rynie/Umzinto offramp, taking the High Flats/Ixopo Road.

The turn-off to the reserve is about 3km past the town of Umzinto, and 12.5km from the freeway. The Kwamzukwa gate itself is 6km from this turn-off.

OPPOSITE: To the experienced rider, singletrack is the very essence of mountain biking.

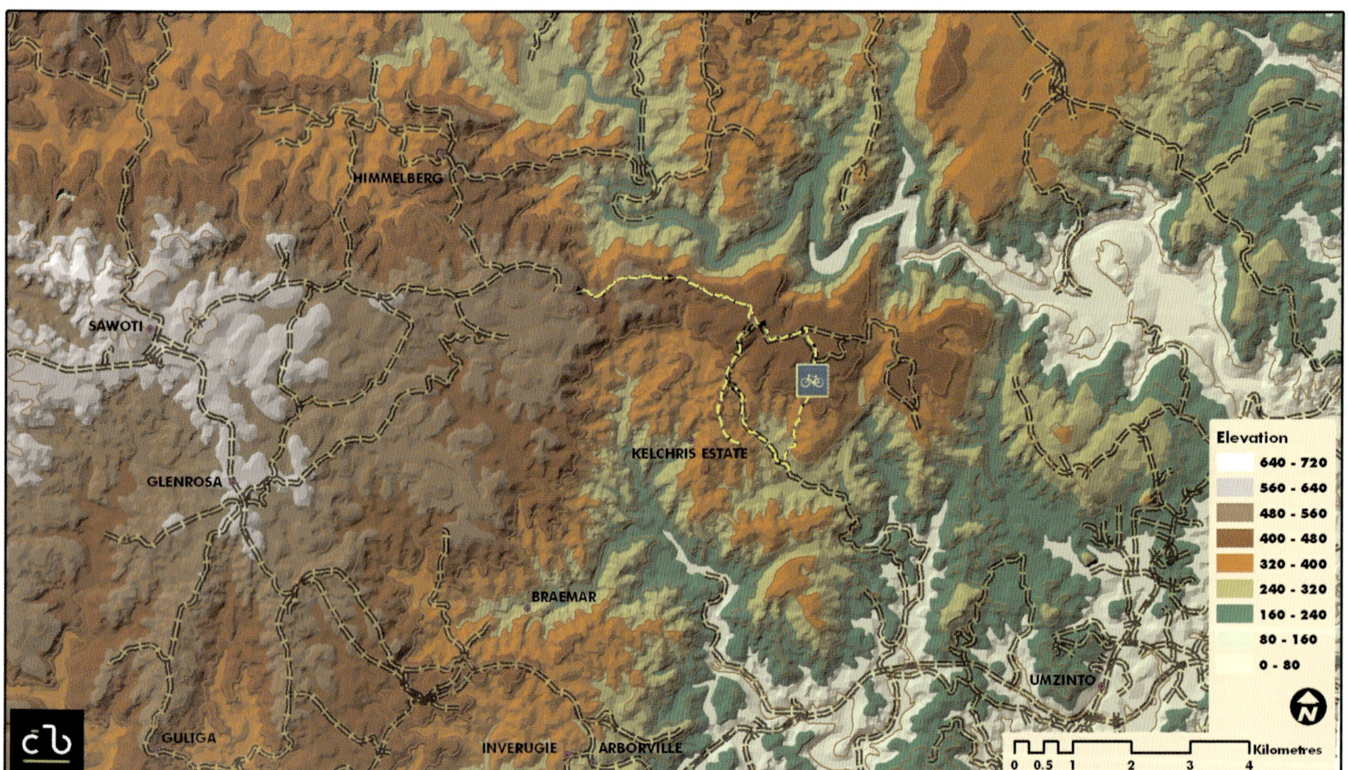

Best ride

For starters we rode a very scenic singletrack that is actually a short cut created by the footwork of staff going between reception and the Kwamzukwa gate. It starts behind the reserve's offices and clings to the contour for several hundred metres before becoming quite steep and heading straight down the hill, where you will have to dismount and carry your bike across the stream. Watch out for slippery rocks, particularly when wearing clip-in cycling shoes. Immediately, a leg-crunching climb goes up and over the side of the hill via a cluster of indigenous forest where slippery roots will test your bike-handling abilities.

More fast, sweeping singletrack will catapult you down the next hill, where you need to cross the Umhlangwe River. There is a basic wooden bridge which can be walked or ridden, but it is extremely slippery when wet and you may

HOW TO BE ENVIRONMENTALLY RESPONSIBLE ON THE BIKE

1) **Ride on open trails only** – do not ride in an area that is closed to cyclists.

2) **Control your bicycle** – keep your speed on descents and braking under control, unless you are racing at an organized event.

3) **Always yield on the trail** – a bicycle is silent, and it is very easy to surprise slow-moving hikers or equestrians when approaching them from behind. Slow down to their speed and ask if you may pass, or wait on the side of the trail until they have passed you.

4) **Never scare animals** – respect all wildlife.

5) **Leave no trace** – take whatever you brought with you back home. Be proactive, and carry a plastic bag with you to pick up other people's rubbish to dispose of appropriately.

6) **Plan ahead** – do not become so engrossed in the ride that you forget to anticipate what is happening on the trail. In a broader context, join your local MTB club, and work with land managers to facilitate your enjoyment and transport of your mountain bike.

unexpectedly and intimately examine the watercourse a few metres below. Another very short, steep climb will deposit you onto the main access road a few hundred metres from the main gate.

This is the turn-around point for the first section, and you can now cycle back up the steep climb to the office area along smooth dirt road. Take time to bathe your eyes in the sea of green all around you and don't miss the road to the scenic viewpoint. This 3km detour on the way to the offices is a fast rollercoaster jeep track along a spur to the viewpoint, where you can take a break and recover for the next long climb ahead to the top part of the reserve. Carry on climbing until you see a sign indicating the 4x4 trail. At this point you can go straight and short change yourself, or follow the challenging 4x4 trail around the back of the reserve for a special treat. Here you are guaranteed the most outstanding, panoramic views over the Mphamambanyoni River and the Indian Ocean. The 4x4 route is an out-and-back ride, so you will have to turn around at the perimeter fence and return to the reception area.

When to go

April to September is definitely the best time as the summers here get uncomfortably hot and humid.

Other rides

On the KwaZulu-Natal North Coast there is **Camp Shaka**, 70km from Durban and 30km inland from Umhlali. The camp offers rustic accommodation beneath the cool, moist canopy of a magnificent expanse of indigenous forest and you have a choice of reed and thatch huts or wooden bungalows, accessible only by foot. The cycling around here is demanding, since the only way out from Camp Shaka is up. For cycling tourists there is a scenic 35km cruise to Ballito on well-maintained dirt roads, and quiet tarred roads all the way down to a dip in the sea. For the off-road rider there's a 7km jeep track from the camp down the valley that is sandwiched between cane fields and a gum plantation,

OPPOSITE: Relax: you're in the bush now.
ABOVE: Bicycles' use as a mode of environmentally responsible means of transport cannot be disputed.

eventually joining up with the dirt road to Umhlali. Rock climbing and team adventure weekends can be arranged. Serviced guesthouses available. (032) 947-9334 (after hours).

The **Kenneth Stainbank Nature Reserve** lies 13km from the Durban CBD. An extension of the D'Moss green lung in the southwestern suburbs of Durban, Stainbank has become a refuge for the city's mountain bikers as well as a rare species of Natal owl and migratory birds. There is a 5–7km lap circuit; you don't have to ride the technical bits. There are picnic spots, safe parking and controlled access so you can relax and just enjoy the ride. This reserve is noted for its facilitation of disabled visitors with a 400m concrete self-guided trail, (031) 469-2807.

The South Coast also offers the **Umtamvuna MTB Trail**. It is strategically positioned on the provincial border and cycling visitors are welcome to ride from Clearwater Chalets on top of the Umtamvuna Gorge looking out over Pondoland. This ride is only 7.5km inland from Port Edward and cyclists have a choice of custom-marked and mapped 6/10/14/22km mountain bike trails that go through a relaxing, yet challenging variety of indigenous forest, footpaths and numerous watercrossings. Chalet guests ride for free, day visitors by appointment only. Bikes are available to hire and guided off-road rides into the Wild Coast region can be arranged. (039) 311-1130.

June sees the annual Sardine Classic. All proceeds go to KZN Wildlife. Call Helena van der Merwe on 083 657-5711 for more information on this event.

Off-the-bike entertainment

Self-catering, secluded accommodation is available at Vernon Crookes Nyengelezi Camp, which consists of a 10-bed tree house, and five two-bed rondavels. Beautiful picnic sites for day visitors and guests.

In keeping with the wilderness philosophy of KZN Wildlife, there is a pristine area reserved within Vernon Crookes. This may only be viewed by appointment, and then only when accompanied by a field guide. It lies in a massive, rugged valley and you walk down through indigenous scrub along an old road to view gold mine workings of the past.

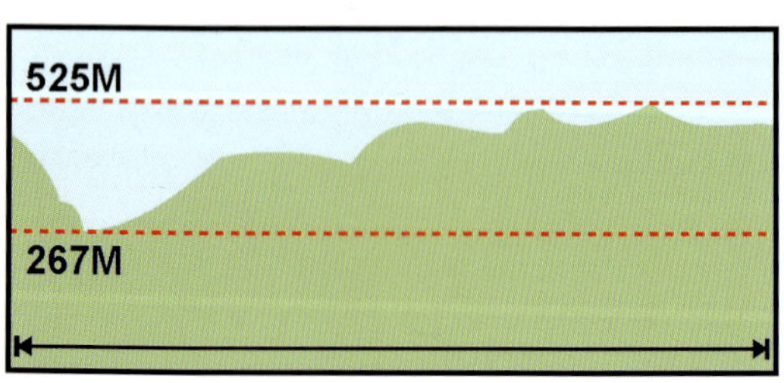

FAST FACTS

ROUTE
A hub ride – series of return rides from the offices.

TRAFFIC
Shared with 4x4s on jeep tracks and pedestrians on footpaths.

ATTRACTIONS
A green feast for the eyes. Winding watercourses and deep valleys with the sea always on the horizon.

START POINT
Reception at Vernon Crookes:
30°27.128' South, 30°60.699' South

FACILITIES
Picnic sites with ablutions; a map of the reserve is available from reception.

ENTRY FEE
Entrance fee payable.
Day visitors are welcome.

CONTACT NUMBERS
Vernon Crookes Nature Reserve:
(039) 974-2222
vcrookes@kznwildlife.com
Accommodation: KZN Wildlife:
(033) 845-1000
www.kznwildlife.com
Map info: Craig Beech at cbeech@mighty.co.za

BEWARE OF
Fall potential on slippery surfaces – take care on river crossings.

THUMBS DOWN
Mountain biking has a delicate toehold in only a handful of nature reserves managed by KZN Wildlife. Information about legal rides can be very hard to get hold of. It would be great if visitors to the reserves in KZN could have ready access to such information.

OPPOSITE: Beautiful subtropical vegetation and large hills provide scenery unique to the KwaZulu-Natal coastal regions and make this a truly special ride. Vernon Crookes Nature Reserve is a good example of a reserve's long-term commitment to ensure that there will always be timeless places where people can freely immerse themselves in the wilderness.

MOST HELLISH RIDE

Province: Western Cape Closest Towns: Prince Albert/Oudtshoorn Distance: 59km (one way)

The contorted sandstone strata of this ancient Cape Fold range form an unforgettable backdrop to a magnificent mountain biking experience.

SWARTBERG

The Swartberg Pass that links the Little and the Great Karoo between the towns of Oudtshoorn and Prince Albert, rates as one of South Africa's most spectacular and dramatic mountain roads. With rugged, soaring cliffs rising up on either side, this was the final masterpiece of Thomas Bain – constructed with the help of convict labour between 1879 and 1887. As you crank into the teeth of gravity, the Karoo scrub slowly gives way to swaying stands of fynbos, combining a diverse range of ecosystems ensconced within the Swartberg Nature Reserve. Just beyond the apex of the pass, the road to Gamkaskloof turns west along a grinding ride into Die Hel, a name directly linked to the tortuous journey into this hidden and fertile valley where an isolated farming community prospered for nearly a century.

These hardy folk loved their remote paradise and named it Gamkaskloof, but the lure of the outside world proved too much once a road finally reached their valley in 1962. One by one the inhabitants left for the outside world and Die Hel once again lay dormant until it was eventually incorporated into the Swartberg Nature Reserve. Under the auspices of Cape Nature Conservation, Gamkaskloof became a National Heritage site in 1997, with many of the houses now restored as self-catering cottages. If you plan on mountain biking into Die Hel, expect most of the riding to be on reasonably good gravel surfaces, albeit along extremely steep gradients for long sections of the route.

PREVIOUS PAGE: The Swartberg switchback curves and swerves as a lone rider battles it out with gravity.
LEFT: Arid Karoo scrub gives way to mountain fynbos as you ascend along the Swartberg Pass.

60%
DISTANCE – A long 59km ride

60%
TIME IN THE SADDLE – 4–7 hours

50%
DANGER – water crossings, steep downhills, loose gravel

50%
TECHNICAL LEVEL – Reasonably good gravel roads

90%
GRADIENT – Severe climbs along hill upon hill upon hill

60%
DIFFICULTY RATING – Difficult

Rated by Jacques Marais

The setting

Crank back through time into a geological wonder world where the convoluted shapes of sedimentary layers offer a window on a prehistoric age when the supercontinent of Gondwanaland heaved and bucked under the torment of colossal terrestrial forces.

As you ascend from the alluvial plains into the sandstone and shale ridges, the remarkable diversity of the vegetation will become evident, with Karoo-, Renoster- and Spekboomveld changing seamlessly into endless expanses of mountain fynbos.

Numerous bulb species, beautiful succulents such as the endemic *Bijlia cana*, mountain aloe, melkbos, waboom protea and cabbage tree are but a few of the 600-plus plant species that flourish within the various vegetation zones.

Although rare, leopard and lynx still roam the broken Swartberg topography, preying on chacma baboons (their favourite quarry) and an abundant supply of klipspringer, rhebok, duiker and grysbok. More than 150 bird species have been listed in Gamkaskloof and close-up sightings of regal black eagles are not uncommon.

How to get there

Prince Albert is situated approximately 400km from Cape Town along the N1 highway. Turn off onto the R407 exactly 87km after passing through Laingsburg, then continue along the Prince Albert road until you reach this perfectly preserved little Victorian village. To get to the beginning of the pass, follow the R407 for another 3km and then turn right onto the R328, a gravel road climbing through the Swartberg Mountains towards Oudtshoorn.

Best ride

There can only be one. Since 1893, when George Boulton and Gabriel van der Westhuizen first raced their bicycles from Prince Albert to Oudtshoorn and back in 12 hours,

the Swartberg Pass has attained an undeniable mystique amongst members of South Africa's mountain biking clan.

Set off from Prince Albert along the R407 to Oudtshoorn for a gentle tarmac cruise until you reach the turn-off to the Swartberg Pass on the R328 to your right (3km). The gentle gradient continues for another two kilometres along the gravel road until you enter the narrow poort, but from here gravity kicks in with maximum intent. The next 12km will see you climb more than a thousand metres (with the gradient occasionally hitting a calf-crunching 1:8) past Eerste- and Tweedewater towards Malvadraai (9km). By the time you hit Blikstasie (the Old Jail, just on halfway into the climb), you'll be locked into granny gear with the dry-stone walling of ZigZag Bend looming dishearteningly high against the horizon. Beyond these switchback curves, the gradient becomes less severe as you ascend towards Teeberg and finally slam into a short but sweet downhill run towards the Gamkaskloof turn-off (17km).

Don't kid yourself into thinking you're home and dry now, for a gruelling 40km ride awaits before you even arrive in Die Hel. Although you have conquered the longest of the climbs, many an uphill still awaits as you thump and shudder along the gnarly Gamkaskloof track. This is a ride that shouldn't be rushed, so take the time to revel in the fields of ericas, bristly stands of restios and ancient waboom proteas.

In winter, you'll be looking at several water crossings. Mist or rain is often prevalent, even during the high summer months, so keep your eyes on the road as you helter-skelter deeper and deeper into the bowels of the hulking Swartberg.

Three major climbs await as you cycle along the high road towards Eland's Pass, the road that swoops down into Die Hel. Worst of these is the final ride up Heartbreak Hill (named thus by the organisers of the To Hell and Back MTB Challenge), a constantly rising, never-ending, cramp-inducing, 5km son-of-a-berg awaiting you with malice at the 50km mark.

To me, this climb poses more of a challenge than the Swartberg Pass itself; for by now your legs are buggered and you'll have been in the saddle for around four hours, so it takes true grit to ride this one all the way to the top.

OPPOSITE: This turn-off points the way to a long, tortuous ride into Die Hel.

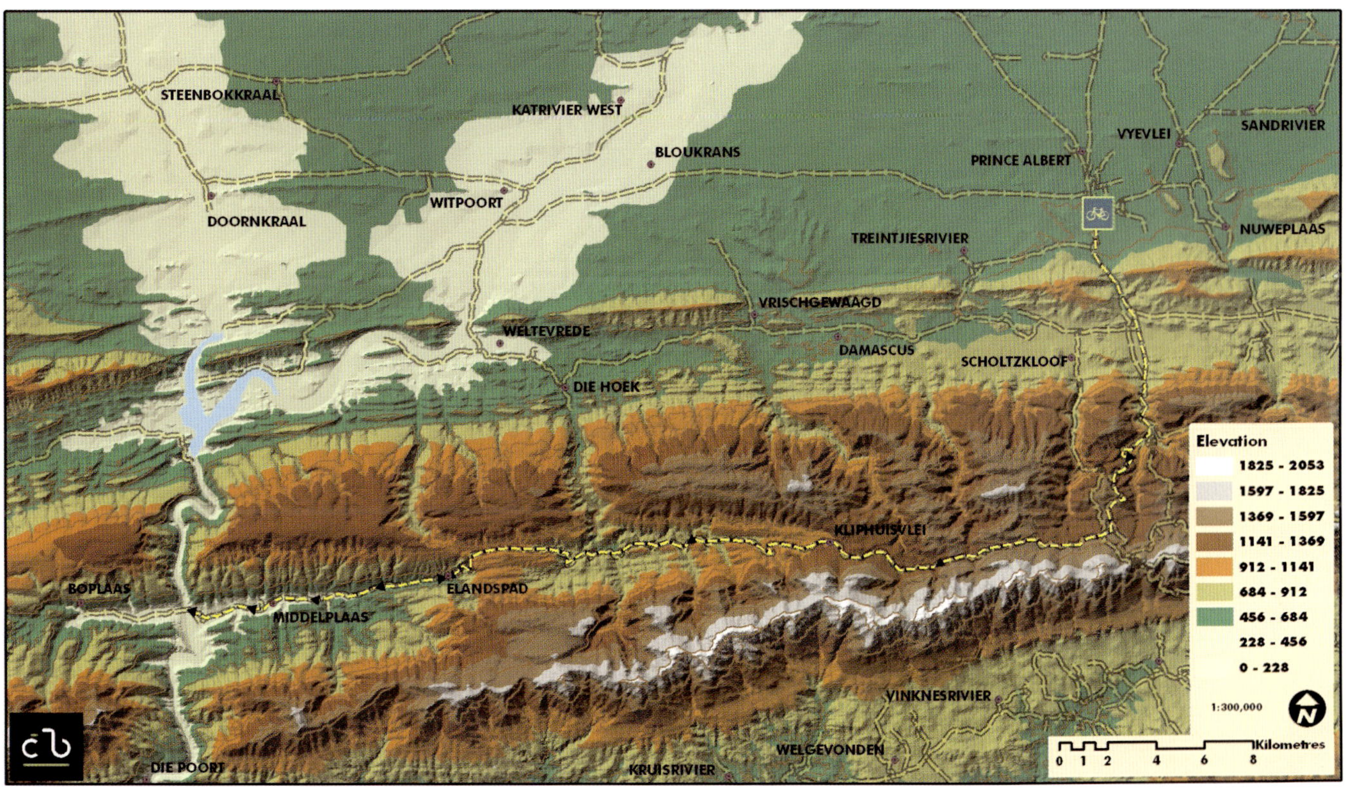

But when you finally summit, the awe-inspiring view along the gravel zigzag of the Eland's Pass blasting down into the verdant valley below will make it all worthwhile. With the camp site at the entrance to Gamkaskloof at an altitude of 560m, a drop of nearly one thousand metres over a distance of four kilometres will be staring you in the face. Take a couple of deep breaths, saddle up and get ready to kick some big mountain butt as you hit the home run and relish the suddenly abundant supply of gravity. After what may arguably rate as the hardest climb of your life, this will indeed seem like divine retribution.

PLEASE NOTE: At the time of writing, Cape Nature Conservation had just opened another off-road route specifically aimed at 4x4 vehicles and mountain bikes. This promises to be even tougher than the regular Gamkaskloof route and will certainly appeal to hard-core riders. There is a fee payable per rider.

When to go

Although Gamkaskloof itself boasts a subtropical microclimate, the summers tend to be severe and generally dry despite the occasional thunderstorm. It is, however, significantly colder in the higher lying mountainous areas, with heavy winter rains and sporadic snowfalls often making the roads impassable. March to May or September to November is probably your best bet for a visit. (The annual two-day, two-way To Hell and Back MTB Challenge usually happens in November.)

Other rides

If you're keen to experience the Swartberg scenery without the vertiginous climbs, opt for a more relaxed cruise down

FAST FACTS

ROUTE
A gravel road from Prince Albert, up the Swartberg Pass and into Gamkaskloof.

TRAFFIC
A dusty straggle of tourist cars and microbuses also checking out the scenery.

ATTRACTIONS
Spectacular rock strata; sublime fynbos; historic surroundings; and the friendliest locals on the planet.

START POINT
The T-junction of the R328 with the R407: 33°15.757' South, 22°02.849' East

FACILITIES
Die Hel camp site with ablution facilities, several self-catering cottages, no fuel.

ENTRY FEE
There is a nominal entry fee to Gamkaskloof.

CONTACT NUMBERS
Swartberg Nature Reserve: (044) 279-1739
sberg.cnc.karoo@pixie.co.za
www.capenature.org.za
Prince Albert Tourism Bureau: (023) 541-1366
princealberttourism@intekom.co.za
www.princealbert.org.za or www.patourism.co.za
Map info: Craig Beech at cbeech@mighty.co.za

BEWARE OF
Extreme changes of temperature – the top of the pass is much cooler than the village or the valley.

THUMBS DOWN
It is hot, sweaty as hell and bloody hard work. At best you'll be swopping secondary gravel for 4x4 roads, so not much in the way of dedicated mountain biking trials.

to the **Gamkapoort Dam**. Imagine a few short and sweet ascents along a moderate route lined with loogbossie, mimosa, wild olive, karee, ghwarri and aloe. Throw in a stunning selection of raptors and other birds, plus a few rocky outcrops with klipspringers silhouetted against the powder-blue Karoo sky and it's ride on! Despite a rocky river crossing over the Gamka and a few sandy patches, the 39km (one way) route down to the dam is an enjoyable excursion and a good choice for a family ride. Even better, get someone to drive a vehicle down and lay out a picnic ready for your arrival.

There is no way you can leave the region without notching up a pukka Great Karoo ride with windmills and doringdraad and candyfloss sheep grazing upon plains stretching beyond eternity. It will, however, mean heading back onto the N1 and through Beaufort West before turning left towards **Hillandale Farm**. Nestling in the folds of the Nuweveld Mountains along a divisional road to Victora

OPPOSITE: Proteas and high altitude fynbos flourish within the protected confines of Gamkaskloof.
BELOW: Pack a shell jacket to help you cope with the extreme temperature variations of the Swartberg Mountains and Gamkaskloof.

West, this gracious and historic Karoo farm offers some great off-road riding along a number of farm roads and three dedicated 4x4 tracks.

Trail distances vary between 34km and 64km and you will have to negotiate sandy riverbeds, deep erosion dongas, steep ascents and gravel downhills. Farm gates and river crossings are numbered and a detailed trail map, available from the farmhouse, will assist you in navigating the rambling Karoo roads. Local fauna include springbok, fallow deer, kudu, the critically endangered riverine rabbit and more than 80 species of bird, including purple heron, spoonbill and black stork.

HOW TO BE KING IN THE MOUNTAINS

1) **Spin doctor** – conserve your energy while ascending along a steep gradient by riding in a low gear, using a consistent spinning motion rather than a pumping crank.

2) **Cramping your style** – avoid cramps by regularly standing up in your saddle to improve blood flow and by adding a replacement electrolyte mix to whatever you drink.

3) **Sit back and relax** – riser bars will allow you occasionally to change the position in which you're sitting, thus avoiding possible back pain or spasms.

4) **Slide rule** – the steep gradient along the downhill sections might tempt you to feed unnecessarily on speed; be mindful of the mega-drops on the pass.

5) **Bum rap** – four or five hours in the saddle equals a sore butt. Minimise damage by wearing padded cycling pants, opting for a full suspension bike or seat post and making sure your saddle settings are spot-on.

Facilities are top-notch. There is lovely self-catering accommodation in a big, historic farmhouse, extremely comfortable fully catered accommodation right in the homestead and camping at the Big Weir Camp with full ablutions, places to braai and stone huts.

Off-the-bike entertainment

Prince Albert, a little gem of preserved period architecture snuggling up to the foothills of the Swartberg ranges, and the Klein Karoo as a whole offer a superb getaway option for the whole family. Choice restaurants, earthy craft shops, avant-garde galleries and elegant accommodation establishments solicit your attention along a main road that is dominated by the historic facade of the laid-back Swartberg Hotel. Don't miss the Olive Festival (April) or the winter Witblits Festival (August), two events that truly make this town come alive.

Once you venture out into the mountains, the menu of action options is endless: hike the amazing Swartberg Trail, visit working fruit and olive farms, do the 56km return 4x4 route into Die Hel, walk in the footsteps of dinosaurs while hunting fossils or simply chill while tucking into a springbok pie at Sampie's Plaasstal.

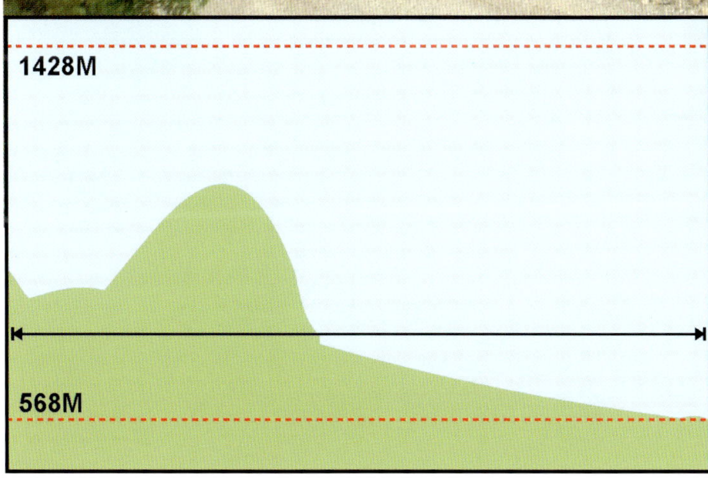

OPPOSITE: High speed cruising is possible along the good gravel road leading up to the Swartberg Pass.
ABOVE: The dramatic entrance from Prince Albert bangs you right into the bowels of the mountains.

BEST BUSHVELD RIDE

Province: Limpopo **Closest Town:** Mokopane (Potgietersrus) **Distance:** 7–24km

...with optional diversions off the beaten track to introduce exciting jeep and singletrack up challenging kloofs and through gaps between the granite outcrops...

THABAPHASWA

BLACK

Thabaphaswa may be somewhat of a tongue twister, so break it down to make more sense: 'Thaba' means mountain in Sotho, and 'Phaswa' means Nguni cattle. Put them together, visit the place and you will see how the shadows and highlights on the rocks of the mountains are reminiscent of the markings on the farm's rare Nguni cattle. Deon Richter ran the Development Bank of South Africa until he bought the farm Groenkom in 1994. He applied the same meticulousness that comes from running a major bank and invested his wealth of professional experience into creating Thabaphaswa – and then sharing it with like-minded people as an authentic African ecotourism experience.

Passion infuses the atmosphere at Thabaphaswa. There is a passion for the environment, and a commitment to all things intrinsically South African. There is minute attention to detail, from the unique outdoor dwellings to the indigenous chickens strutting around the farmyard. Mountain biking is no exception, and the off-road cycling trails have been personally tested by Heinrich Richter, son of Deon and Ankie.

In the words of *Bicyling SA* editor Sean Badenhorst: 'Eating and sleeping is just something you unfortunately have to do, in between riding here.' Expect to experience what is surely a monument to the sport of off-road cycling.

PREVIOUS PAGE: A fast sweeping descent will satisfy those riders with preference for speed, but be aware of farm gates across the roads, and wash-outs from rainwater. LEFT: Majestic valleys make this an impressive landscape, typical of Limpopo Province's bushveld.

40%
DISTANCE – 7–24km so you can dress this ride up or down

40%
TIME IN THE SADDLE – About 1–3 hours

30%
DANGER – Lightning; occasional thorns

30%
TECHNICAL LEVEL – Fall potential if you push it

60%
GRADIENT – Very steep in places

40%
DIFFICULTY RATING - Moderate

Rated by Herman Mills

The setting

Domed granite mountains endemic to the area are reminiscent of the Matopos near Bulawayo in Zimbabwe. From the Thabaphaswa Mountain, a geological giant that at 1 700m often has its head in the clouds, one can see the nearby town and, if you know where to look, the World Heritage site of the Makapan Caves. The mountain is an important landmark to all the people of this area, and for centuries travellers and traders have used it to get their bearings. All this abundance of exposed rock, however, does attract its fair share of lightning.

Vegetation like kanniedood, paperbark cork and wild fig trees can be found clustered about the base of huge granite rocks or doing their bit for erosion by prizing apart cracks in the rocks with their roots.

None of the wild game that you encounter here has been introduced. In line with the commitment to a genuine ecotourism experience, what you see is what has always been here. The large variety of animals include leopard, baboon (the leopard's favourite dish), duiker, klipspringer, jackal, warthog, brown hyena, rhebok, and black eagle. Since this is a working cattle farm, the unspoken rule with regards to farm gates applies: if it was closed, then close it behind you, and, if it was open, leave it open. Littering can cause the loss of livestock, so carry out with you what you carried in and leave only tracks behind.

How to get there

Thabaphaswa lies 215km from Pretoria (Tshwane) and 270km from Johannesburg. Take the N1 North, and exit at the Nyl Toll Plaza. Turn left onto the Roedtan/Marble Hall Road, and travel 1km until you reach the T-junction with the R101. Turn right to Mokopane (Potgietersus) and travel for 10km. Go straight through the town and look for the road to Percy Fyfe Nature Reserve on the left. Travel 8km on tar, 3.5 km on dirt. 600m after the bridge you will see a thatched homestead on the left. Turn left here, and the entrance gate to Thabaphaswa is 2km further. A map of the trails is available and they are all well signposted.

Best ride

Thanks to its geology, Thabaphaswa has very scenic and some rather challenging trails. The ride featured here is basically a circular route, with optional diversions off the

beaten track to introduce exciting jeep and singletrack up challenging kloofs and through gaps between the granite outcrops that cover the farm.

Although the main route is only about 7km in length and not that technical, there is enough sand, gravel and rocks to make it the ideal route to introduce novice cyclists to off-road riding, and perfect for a mellow, late afternoon ride with the family. Since the farm is fully fenced you cannot get completely lost and the map provided by the Richters gives ample directions and indicators of where to go, and where to turn back home. At the same time, all of the hiking and biking trails are beautifully signposted and make finding your way around very easy.

The start of your ride can be from any of the camps. In our case it was from a point roughly halfway between the Dome Rock Camp and the farm's homestead. A steep little climb around the first and most prominent hill on the farm takes you along smooth and very scenic jeep track into the heart of those mystical giant granite mounds. From here the singletrack veers off the main route up a steep climb (made somewhat technically demanding by the farm's cows) that will give your legs a rude awakening.

After passing through a gate, continue up this climb and enjoy the fascinating trees that are found in this part of the country, like the huge naboom or candelabra growing next to the main track. After another kilometre or two you will be able to rest and grab a quick bite to eat at a stunning lookout point. To get there, you will have to carry the bike for a 100 metres or so, but the setting is worth it.

On your way back to the main trail, pay attention to a magnificent specimen of wild fig tree to your right growing amongst the rocks just off the singletrack. A fast sweeping descent will satisfy those riders with preference for speed, but be aware of farm gates across the roads, and wash-outs from rainwater (as one of us found out the painful way when he overcooked it on a middelmannetjie and made close acquaintance with the local geology – followed by a lone, airborne bike trying to reunite itself with its rider).

Depending on your fitness level you can either carry on exploring the singletrack until you have covered everything the farm has to offer (you will do approximately 30km) or cut the ride shorter by getting back onto the main road, working your way back to the main camp and homestead.

Longer rides can be done in the area for those who cannot sit still, but at this stage a nice cold beverage of some sort while sitting on a large granite dome with a good view would be the perfect opportunity to relax and listen to the multitude of bird sounds in this unique piece of the bushveld.

When to go

The bushveld climate means that the trail can be ridden throughout the whole year. This property is surrounded by mountains, thus ensuring mild temperatures. Summer temperatures range from 17–29°C and winter sees them anywhere between 6 and 22°C.

Other rides

The **Percy Fyfe Nature Reserve** offers a tough 40km return ride using the railway servitude road from Thabaphaswa to the Percy Fyfe entrance gate. Add another 20km if you would like to include a circuit inside the reserve itself. (015) 491-5678

The **Nylsvley Nature Reserve** is situated 10km outside Mookgophong (Naboomspruit) and consists partly of a grassy flood plain formed by the Nyl River. This is a birding paradise, with around 400 species making their homes here. The rainy season turns the reserve into a wet wonderland when the perennial flood plain fills up and water birds flock here in their thousands.

The mountain bike riding can be rather sandy in the western section of the reserve; otherwise it is hardpack and bushveld – perfect for all levels of rider. Camping is available in the reserve. (014) 743-1074

Annual MTB events in this area include the Lion Man MTB Challenge (35/80km) in the Mabilingwe Game Reserve near Bela-Bela (Warmbaths) during May, (014) 736-9000. August sees the Mazda Drifter MTB Development Race at Stanford College in Magoebaskloof and, in November, Stanford also hosts the Magoebaskloof Classic at Stanford College (35/75km).

Off-the-bike entertainment

Thabaphaswa itself offers hiking, rock climbing, swimming in the farm dam, game viewing and bird watching. The Mokopane area is one of South Africa's richest agricultural spots and produces wheat, tobacco, cotton, beef, maize, peanuts and citrus. The Zebediela Citrus estate, 55 km to the southeast, is one of the biggest citrus farms in the southern hemisphere.

Makapansgat, just 11.5km north of Mokopane, consists of huge limestone caves that have yielded some of the oldest hominid remains ever known, dating back 3.3 million years. Makapansgat may be viewed by appointment only.

The old Klipskool in Mokopane is now home to the Arend Dieperink Museum, where exhibits of multi-cultural artefacts from Limpopo Province are on display. Also of interest are the National Zoological Gardens.

More information on the area can be obtained from the Mogalakwena C.T.A. Contact them on (015) 491-8458 or sabek@mweb.co.za

FAST FACTS

ROUTE
An easy hub loop of about 7km, with more challenging diversions branching off. A mixture of smooth dirt roads, rough jeep track and exciting singletrack.

TRAFFIC
Cattle and farm gates, possibly baboons.

ATTRACTIONS
A unique ecofriendly cycling experience between a crowd of giant rocks.

START POINT
Thabaphaswa:
24°05.680 South, 29°04.397 East

FACILITIES
A variety of self-catering accommodation is available. There is also a tented camp site where you can stay, or bring your own tent and caravan if you like.

ENTRY FEE
Entry fee payable for day visitors.

CONTACT NUMBERS
Reservations through Jacana Country Homes and Trails: (012) 346-3550
info@jacanacollection.co.za
www.jacanacollection.co.za
MTB Skills Clinics are conducted by Fritz Pienaar Cycles at Thabaphaswa: (012)460-2385
www.adventurezone.co.za
Map info: Craig Beech at cbeech@mighty.co.za

BEWARE OF
Lots of lightning at Thabaphaswa.
The occasional thorn might puncture your tyres.

THUMBS DOWN
Although a sufficient map is provided, better signposting along the route (especially on the singletrack) would be great to prevent getting lost and having to double back.

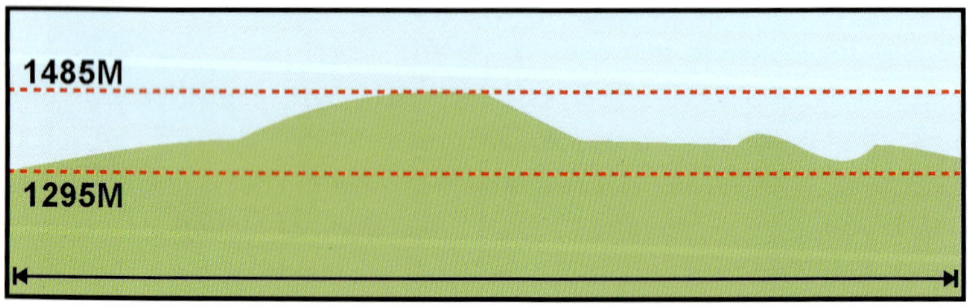

ABOVE LEFT: Don't overdo it – there are plenty of scenic recovery spots dotted along the trail. Another option would be sitting on a large granite dome with a good view.
OPPOSITE: Thanks to its geology, Thabaphaswa has very scenic and some rather challenging trails. There is therefore no shortage of steep, hard climbs to challenge riders of all levels.

HOW TO DEAL WITH PUNCTURE PROBLEMS

1) **Never put a spare tube** back into a tyre without running your hand along the inside tyre wall to check for barbs sticking through.

2) **Use tyre liners.** Consider inserting slime, but if money is tight, just bear in mind that if you get an impact puncture and the hole is too big for the slime to fill, you have to throw your tube away because slime will not allow you to patch it. Another option is tubeless tyres, but you will have to weigh up the pros and cons. Also try inflating your tyres quite hard if you are going to a thorny, rocky area.

3) **Don't pull out thorns** during a ride, no matter how tempting. The thorn is sometimes keeping a perforation in your tube sealed. Often you can ride around for days with an assortment of thorns bristling in between your knobblies with no deflation.

BEST DOWNHILL

Province: Western Cape **Closest Town:** Cape Town **Distance:** 18.4km

The amber glow of the late afternoon sun slanting through tall trees; pine needles sizzling beneath your wheels... This is probably as close as you will ever get to riding the Holy Trail.

TOKAI

Vans
MANTRA
Giro
MANTRA

Ask any mountain biker what makes a ride and you can bet good money on the word singletrack popping up somewhere in their answer. No wonder then Tokai rates right up there on the A-list of local riders as one of South Africa's must-do Holy Trails.

This MTO Forestry administered area (currently in the process of being incorporated into the world-famous Table Mountain National Park) constitutes everything held in high esteem by the fat track tribe: a calf-crunching, profanity-inducing mother of a dirt track climb; a scenic, natural setting incorporating indigenous forest, well-maintained plantations and slopes covered in endemic Cape fynbos; fast-track forest downhills bombing along sweeping gravel curves and enough singletrack sections to induce yee-ha hollering in even the most jaded of gearheads.

PREVIOUS PAGE: An early morning mountain biker bombs the Table Mountain range while Cape Town basks in the warm light of dawn.
LEFT: Hard-core downhill riders on long-travel shock machines lay claim to many of the gnarlier sections of the Tokai trail.

30%
DISTANCE – Short at 18.4km

30%
TIME IN THE SADDLE – Approximately 2 hours

70%
DANGER – Sharp corners, fallen trees, drop-offs, mega fall potential

60%
TECHNICAL LEVEL – Tree roots, rocky drop-offs, pine needles

60%
GRADIENT – Continual climb followed by a hard-core downhill

50%
DIFFICULTY RATING – Moderate to difficult

Rated by Jacques Marais

The setting

Any forest is a thing of beauty, but the Cape montane variety blanketing the majestic slopes of Table Mountain is especially spectacular. Despite severe deforestation by early colonists, the declaration of sections of the Peninsula as a nature reserve in the mid-nineteenth century has ensured the protection of luxuriant stands of Cape beech, yellowwood and wild almond. Ravines, gulleys and stream beds erupt in a profusion of evergreen shrubs and feathery ferns, while velvety coatings of moss and phat fungi put in regular appearances during the Western Cape's so-called winter 'Green Season'.

With much of the Tokai plantation constantly being harvested (and with some sections cleared in an effort to rid the Cape Peninsula of alien vegetation), pristine expanses of fynbos are being reclaimed along much of Tokai's upper slopes. Here you may cycle amongst pincushion proteas, delicate ericas, underbrush and swaying stands of restios while sugarbirds, peregrine falcons and orange-breasted sunbirds cruise the skies. Chacma baboon, caracal, small-spotted genet and porcupine are just a few of the mammal species to have found refuge here.

How to get there

From Cape Town, follow the M3 highway (locals call it the Blue Route) for 20km in the direction of Cape Point. Keep an eye out for the off-ramp to Tokai on your left, turning right to cross under the highway towards the mountain until you reach the traffic circle (2km). Continue straight across towards Tokai Manor, turn left after just more than a kilometre and then follow the road to your right and into the parking area at the arboretum.

Best ride

Pedal off from the entrance gate at the Tokai Arboretum, ascending along a gentle climb through the lush lower reaches of the plantation.

This moderate incline soon becomes a steep jeep track that climbs through sections of plantation which have recently been cleared. Although track conditions are reasonable, you might have to negotiate the odd section of rocky gravel, and

OPPOSITE: Proteas, ericas and restios line scenic trails along the upper sections of the Tokai Forest.
Below: Main route all the way to Constantiaberg's highest point. For the hairy singletrack switchbacks, take the right fork at the neck

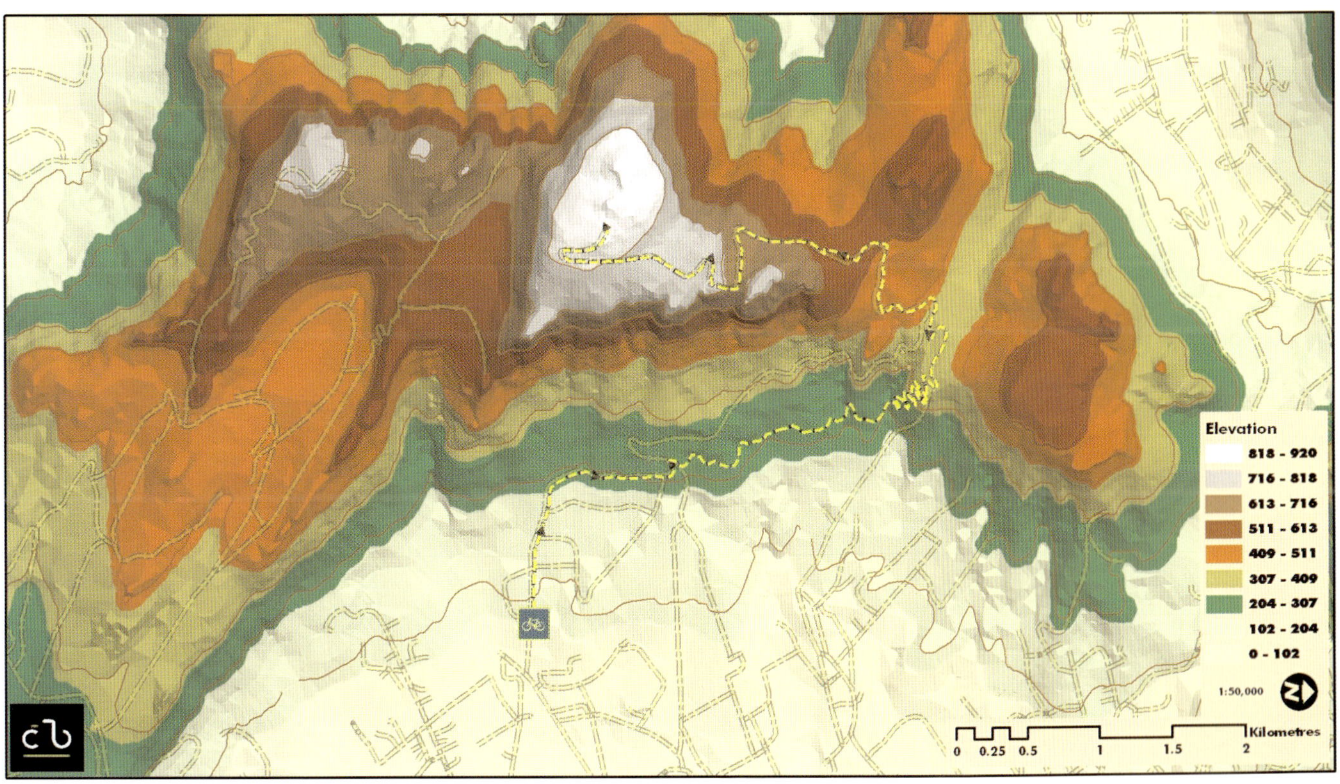

winter rains might unleash anything from mud puddles to fallen trees. Duel it out with gravity for just on 6km before reaching a rudimentary strip of tarmac snaking through a steep fynbos incline towards the Sentech tower.

You'll top out after a further lung-busting 5km to marvel at the breathtaking views across False Bay and out towards the distant Hangklip Point. Get to the base of the looming mast (altitude 928m), bomb the tarmac strip and turn left sharply where you rejoin the gravel to detour onto a switchback trail section sideswiping along the steepening slope below Vlakkenberg Peak (altitude 579m). Then it is back up to the jeep track before dog-legging left into fat track paradise along a spider web of snappy singletrack.

One word of warning; this is baboon country and these furry critters might decide to hog the trail now and then. Treat them with respect; you're a guest in the Table Mountain National Park, which is their rightful home.

Tokai is a rather tricky route, so we've decided to give you a precise breakdown:

(1) Turn right along a good gravel road, cranking away from the Arboretum and ascending into the bottom reaches of the Tokai plantation. At the 300m mark, you'll enter to the left of a gate before continuing along a gradual climb to a fork where you turn right (2.4km).

(2) Pass further forks in the road, but stick to the purple route as indicated on the map you got at the gate, only hitting a sharp left along a bitchy little uphill at 4.5km. The road then T-bones at 5.4km: left climbs towards the Silvermine gate, but you turn right and continue the uphill zigzag until just before the start of the tar road leading up to the radio tower.

(3) Here (7.3km) the road splits left towards the mast, but you opt to go right through a dip and onto the wickedest stretch of singletrack switchback I know (green section on gate map at 8.5km). Hectic pine needle carpet and manic drops, so watch the slippage until you bottom out at 9.8km.

(4) You might want to head back up to bomb the map's blue section of singletrack you missed out on, so return along the pink section back to the top where you'll notice the singletrack dipping down to your right at 12.4km.

(5) Hang on tight, because this fun ride can easily morph into a head-over-heels hospital run if you lose concentration. Basically you're on a switchbitch supertube banging straight across most of the gravel road sections along which you made your way up. Keep an eye out when you dog-leg to your right at the bottom; it will seem as if the singletrack ends against a rutted uphill, but look carefully and you'll find that it continues to your left – about 10m up the slope.

(6) Just on 17km, you'll cross a narrow wooden bridge and find yourself back onto the gravel road where you hang left back towards the arboretum. Relax on the easy home run through the gate and back into the parking area.

HOW TO RIDE A SINGLETRACK

1) **Scan ahead** – keep your eyes focused approximately 5–10 metres ahead of you, giving yourself enough time to prepare for any obstacles along the trail.

2) **Choose your line** – when approaching a gnarly section, select the easiest line and commit to riding it at as high a speed as is safely possible.

3) **Cutting corners** – use your knees and the weight of your body to force the bike into corners, thus allowing you to take them at a higher speed.

4) **Controlled braking** – if necessary, apply brakes before you enter a corner, gearing down and then accelerating through the curve in order to improve your balance.

5) **Going down** – when approaching drop-offs, move your butt right back off the saddle, thus positioning your centre of gravity towards the rear of the bike so that you can avoid going over the handlebars.

When to go

The Cape of Good Trails cooks right through the year. In summer, the lower reaches of the forest cool down the high daytime temperatures, while, in winter, the trees offer some protection from the blasting winds.

Expect the trails to get muddy when the winter rains come down, presenting a perfect opportunity to trail-test those mud tires hanging in the garage.

Other rides

Silvermine, a scenic section of the Table Mountain National Park bordering Tokai to the southwest, runs a close second as far as mountain biking action in the South Peninsula goes. To get there, turn off onto Ou Kaapse Weg (M64) from the Blue Route (M3) and drive in the direction of Noordhoek. After approximately 4km, you will see the turn-off to Silvermine to your right. The ride kicks off about a kilometre further up the

OPPOSITE: Keep an eye out for the 'chicken run' option if you're not keen to commit to those big jumps.

tarmac strip in a small parking area to your right – look out for a sign indicating the start of the MTB route. Psych your bike for a good half hour of climbing along the lower slopes of Constantiaberg (928m) and Noordhoek Peak before you line up the high-speed home run. Maximise your downhill time trail by turning right onto the Ou Wapad slashing down towards the San Michelle turn-off before climbing back up along Ou Kaapse Weg.

But wait, there's more! The section above **Red Hill**, in Simon's Town boasts a rollicking fynbos ride from the Brooklands water treatment plant turn-off on the M66 past the Lewis Gay Reservoir to the Blackhill Road (M6) that links False Bay to the Atlantic Ocean. In summer, the jeep tracks here are as sandy as the Sahara, but winter riding is mighty sweet and dandy.

Some purist dirt gurus might disagree with my final route option, but a leisurely cruise along the narrow tarmac roads of **Cape of Good Hope Nature Reserve** is a fine way to spend a Sunday morning. Take in the views across False Bay and the Atlantic, smell the fynbos fragrance, tip your helmet to a passing parade of bontebok, ostriches and eland, check out Diaz Cross and then have lunch at the Cape Point restaurant before meandering back to the gate.

For more information, check out the TMNP website at www.tmnp.co.za – click on 'downloads' in the pop-up window and you'll find a catalogue of mapped mountain bike routes under the Environmental Management Programme for Recreational Mountain Biking in the TMNP.

Off-the-bike entertainment

Cape Town is fast becoming Africa's premium leisure and adventure playground. The Peninsula wine routes are a must and you can choose from 24 estates that produce world famous wines – the classy wines of the historic Groot Constantia estate are not to be missed.

Surfing is the next big thing to do while in the South Peninsula; give it a shot off Kommetjie along the Atlantic seaboard, or follow in the footsteps of the world's top big wave chargers and brave the waves at Dungeons off Hout Bay.

Boulders Beach offers access to an intriguing, land-based African penguin colony; either cruise the wooden walkways or rent a kayak and paddle onto False Bay to get a better view. And all the while you will be surrounded by the Table Mountain National Park. Short-listed as South Africa's fourth World Heritage site, it encompasses the whole of the Table Mountain range and much of the Peninsula.

FAST FACTS

ROUTE
Return or circular route on singletrack, jeep track plus a 5km tarmac return to the tower.

TRAFFIC
The occasional forestry vehicle; high-speed downhill mountain bikes; horseback riders.

ATTRACTIONS
Superb views over False Bay and the Atlantic Ocean; fynbos vistas; chacma baboons and porcupines.

START POINT
Arboretum gate:
34°03.40' South, 18°24.55' East

FACILITIES
A safe parking area with a security guard, as well as a coffee shop and ablutions.

ENTRY FEE
An entry fee is charged at the gate; an excellent map is also available here.

CONTACT NUMBER
MTO Forestry office: (021) 712-7471
www.tmnp.co.za
Map info: Craig Beech at cbeech@mighty.co.za
Trail maps of other regions, including Grabouw and Stellenbosch also available from Willie Engelbrecht Cycles: (021) 910-0623
wecycles@new.co.za

BEWARE OF
Tree roots and, of course, those baboons are likely to pop up on the trail when you least expect them.

THUMBS DOWN
Weekend mornings get really busy. To get to the downhill singletrack, you need to slog for a good hour along a hard gravel road climb.

OPPOSITE: Tokai forest is a frequent venue for provincial, national and even continental championships.
BELOW: Featured route with singletrack.

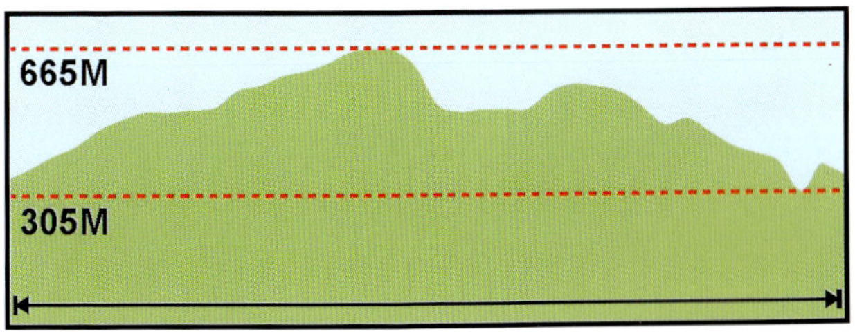

MOST ADVENTUROUS RIDE

Province: Eastern Cape **Closest Towns:** Port St Johns/Coffee Bay **Distance:** 33km

You will be left breathless by the rolling hills and dramatic cliffs that plunge steeply onto a tempestuous shoreline.

WILD COAST

They don't call this 280km stretch of coastline, between the Umtamvuna River in the north and the Kei River in the south, the Wild Coast for nothing. Venture into this heartland of the amaXhosa and you will be left breathless by a landscape that blends rolling hills, dramatic cliffs, estuarine valleys and serene rural villages with a dense tangle of indigenous forests and misty mangrove swamps plunging steeply onto a tempestuous shoreline.

At present, much of the area qualifies as an untamed paradise, but this could soon change if construction goes ahead on a controversial section of toll road that will extend the N2 along what is still today an environmental haven. For the moment, the only way to reach the many pristine bays and tiny hideaways dotting the coast is along pot-holed gravel roads or meandering cattle footpaths. Don't expect the peace and tranquillity to extend to inland towns however – here you will have to face up to the vibrant crush of Africa buzzing at full volume.

The biking varies from hammering along full tilt on never-ending gravel roads or laid-back beach cruising to white knuckle downhills along rutted cattle tracks. There are NO designated routes here, so a certain level of riding skill is required and a sense of adventure is an absolute requirement.

PREVIOUS PAGE: Magnificent views open up behind a lone mountain biker negotiating the cliffs near Coffee Bay.
LEFT: A tranquil coastal forest near Hole-in-the-Wall is the perfect spot for a serene morning ride.

40%

DISTANCE – A moderate 33km

70%

TIME IN THE SADDLE – 5–8 hours

70%

DANGER – Downhill ruts, river crossings, wait-a-bit thorn branches

60%

TECHNICAL LEVEL – Varied: rutted cattle tracks, steep downhills, hiking trail and soft sand

60%

GRADIENT – There are six mean hills, overall climb is moderate

60%

DIFFICULTY RATING – Difficult to extreme *Rated by Jacques Marais*

The setting

A fusion of freshwater rivers, rich inter-tidal zones, pristine beaches, plunging cliffs, tranquil lagoons and rolling grassland contribute to the ecological diversity of the Wild Coast region. Although rural villages dot just about every hilltop, the subsistence farming practised by the locals has left much of the landscape relatively untouched. Overgrazing and the harvesting of indigenous trees for firewood have however left ugly scars in places, but, despite this, more than 40 000 hectares of indigenous forest have survived in dense valleys along the coastline.

The diverse range of biomes stretching along the Wild Coast is home to more than 320 species of bird, including the trumpeter hornbill, rameron pigeon, Cape parrot and Knysna woodpecker. Huge greenbanded swallowtail and striped swordtail butterflies flutter along in the morning breeze, while blue duiker, bushbuck, chacma baboon, samango monkeys and other mammals inhabit the many small nature reserves gracing the coast.

Tidal estuaries, fringed by the planet's southernmost mangrove swamps, offer a safe haven to breeding schools of stumpnose, grunter and kob, while whales, dolphins and monster sharks cruise the Big Blue.

Even more interesting than the diversity of the fauna and flora of the region are the people who live here. Although the inhabitants are generally grouped together as the amaXhosa, they are made up of the distinct groupings of the Thembu, Mpondo, Mpondomise, Bomvana and Mfengu, each with their own set of customs, traditions and beliefs.

How to get there

The N2 from Port Shepstone basically runs parallel to the coast in a north-south direction approximately 50km inland, then curves back towards the sea en route to East London. Secondary tarmac and gravel roads service coastal towns and villages; the smaller the village, the more atrocious you can expect the drive to be.

To get to Hluleka Nature Reserve, drive for 30km along the R61 from Umtata towards Port St Johns before turning right at the sign to this remote little nature reserve.

The 50km there will take you at least an hour along a stretch of road held together by corrugations and potholes, but I assure you that when you see your destination, you will realise that it was well worth the *vasbyt*.

BELOW: Deep ravines and undulating coastal hills make for exciting downhill rides and more than a few gruelling climbs.

Best ride

Let me say it again: do not pitch up somewhere along the Wild Coast and expect to find a demarcated mountain bike trail with secure parking and sparkling ablutions on hand. This is Africa at its most basic (and beautiful), so you'll need to be at your MacGyver best by the time you hit the trail. If you prefer to be pampered, go ride closer to the urban jungle or contact a company like 180 Degree Adventures who run the Wild Coast as a six-day guided MTB trail. There is one other option – once a year, usually during July or August, the Imana Wild Ride from the Kei to Umngazi River is co-ordinated over five days by a band of KwaZulu-Natal mountain bikers.

After chatting to the Imana organisers, the Eastern Cape Tourism Board and a few other riders with on-the-ground knowledge, I decided to cycle along a section of the coast that lies approximately midway between Port Edward and the Kei River Mouth.

My mission was to find a ride that, while exciting and challenging, would not be beyond the abilities of your average weekend cranker. Hazy (I swear I did not inhale the stuff) memories of Hluleka beckoned, so we made a call to start our explorations from this stunning nature reserve in a southerly direction towards the Mbashe River mouth.

Situated about halfway between Coffee Bay and Port St Johns, Hluleka boasts a sheltered beach, tranquil lagoon, stunning indigenous and bamboo forests and a herd of Burchell's zebra grazing the lawns that sprawl below the raised wooden bungalows. An hour or so of exciting riding along the network of hiking trails within the reserve allowed us to tweak the bikes, dice the wildebeest and get a feel for the terrain. Rucksacks were packed, hydration bladders filled, tyre pressure checked, maps laminated, pumps primed, food stocked and the GPS locked and loaded. All systems were go (or so we thought).

An early start saw us setting off along an easy gravel road to the park entrance gate (1.8km), beyond which we slipped left towards the coast along a rutted jeep track that dipped down to a pebble beach (2.7km). A steep double-humped climb (faint jeep track) beckoned to the top of a grassy knoll (3.8km) and it was somewhere during the course of this ascent that the Wild Coast threw its first curve ball at us. I was just priding myself on how well I was doing in keeping pace with Max when he executed a perfect projectile vomit across the handlebars. The reason I'm telling you this is so that you will make sure that you have a backup plan when you're out there. Surprisingly, there is cell phone reception along much of the trail, so take your mobile along (preferably switched off when not in use so you can enjoy the peace and quiet).

Max, who is as headstrong as the local Zebu oxen, insisted on continuing the ride despite suffering several further 'episodes' along the way, but eventually gave up the good fight around Mdumbi Point and agreed to wait for our backup crew. He was diagnosed with tick bite fever a few days later, which goes to show how important it is for you to plan ahead on a trip like this. I would suggest a backup vehicle with a clear rendezvous point along the route or, at the very least, a contact person who could raise the alarm if you do not keep to your proposed ETA.

Back to the route though – once you crest, the jeep track turns into a series of deep ruts dipping down inland. Turn left at 4.1km, heading back towards the ocean and then turn right (4.7km) onto a sweet singletrack trail leading to a stand of mangroves (5.5km). Continue along this trail and you'll reach the hiking trail dipping down towards the Mtakatye River (6km) below. After spotting a big fin patrolling the eddies at Port St Johns the day before, we whistled insistently to attract the attention of a laid-back ferryman, forking out R7 each for the crossing.

BELOW: Hole-in-the-Wall rates as one of the major attractions along the Wild Coast route.
OPPOSITE: Horses, Zebu cattle, diverse fauna and the traditions of the amaXhosa people add even more interest to this amazing ride.

Another stiff climb awaited us as we cranked away from the river towards a small village (also called Mtakatye, at 8.5km) where the closest thing to 'Rehidrate' at the local spaza shop happened to be Stoney's Ginger Beer. From here we blasted along a speedy section of hard-pack in the direction of the ocean, following the road to our right away from Presley Bay (12km) and down onto a stunning stretch of beach. A few hundred metres later gravity kicked in and we got off to push up an extremely steep hill (13.5km) before cruising the contours through a village and onto a section of soft beach sand (17km). Push around the point and hit the beach below Tshani (a great place to swim) and onto a rocky trail leading to Mdumbi River (20 km).

It was low tide, so we could wade across, but by now Max was bonking big time. I left him under a tree and scouted

HOW TO SURVIVE A COASTAL RIVER CROSSING

1) **Local knowledge** – if in doubt as to the safety of a river crossing, speak to the locals and find out where and how they cross. Don't try to wade a river if you feel in any way unsafe.

2) **Ship ahoy!** – if you see a small rowboat, it usually means there is a ferryman in the area. A few loud whistles should eventually rouse him from the dreaded Pondoland Fever.

3) **Pay the ferryman** – negotiate your price before loading the bikes on the boat. Going rate was between R5–R7 at time of writing and I never got the feeling that I was being ripped off.

4) **Walk on water** – depending on the level of the river and tide, the majority of rivers can be waded. Wear shoes to avoid any nasty surprises from stone fish and stingrays though.

5) **Tide table** – always cross during an incoming tide, preferably around half an hour after low tide when it will be at its safest.

6) **Last resort** – if you are faced with a strong current and no other way of crossing, walk upstream first, waterproof your pack and try to float your bike across. Sharks often enter the estuaries, so get as far away from the mouth as you can.

ahead, fortunately discovering a stash of icy cold drinks at Mdumbi Backpackers (21km). Suitably revived, Max crashed in their recreation room to wait for backup, leaving me to bang down onto the beach at Mdumbi Point (22km – the map refers to it as Whale Rock, but none of the locals do). Enjoy 3km of beach cruising to the Mtata River (24.7km – ferry across for a small fee) and then bite the bullet as you slug into a bitch of a jeep track climb.

When you crest the hill, hammer left along the singletrack hiking trail until it drops steeply down into the valley through a scattering of huts (I got chased by dogs here), generally sticking to the low ground until you reach the river (27.5km) at Maputzi Point. Cross along the rocks to the left of the deep pool and haul in all that downhill that you just enjoyed, trudging for just on a kilometre until you summit to gaze out across to the end of the earth (28.5km).

This is how I felt, anyway – all of a sudden, the grassy plateau just plunges away to your left along sheer cliffs charging down onto the foam-splashed rocks far below. The next kilometre of riding is literally and figuratively on the edge, culminating in a giddy view (29.5km) across the Coffee Bay beach. It does however mean that you once again have to head inland in order to circumvent the steep and densely forested ravine gouging down alongside the sheer drop. Follow the contoured cattle footpaths in an anti-clockwise direction, keeping an eye out for a thoroughfare leading onto a track passing just below the garbage dump (31km).

Don't lose it as you head into the gnarly home-run chute skittering down to the hotel gates, turning left through the parking lot and onto the beach (32km). After a few minutes of skimming the high-water mark, you'll be wading across the Nenga River (33km), where ample and shady parking makes for an excellent rendezvous point. Depending on your level of fitness, you're looking at 5 to 8 hours in the saddle up to here, but, if you're keen on another hour or so on the bike, keep going along the gravel road to Hole-in-the-Wall (43km).

When to go

All four seasons at the Wild Coast are special, with the temperate, subtropical climate ensuring good riding throughout the year.

Summer months (October to March) are generally wet, while trails and roads will be drier and therefore more accessible during May and June.

Bear in mind that the annual rainfall is in the region of 750 to 1 400mm, with average maximum daily temperatures of 28°C (January) and 21°C (July) recorded.

Winter is *amakwetha* time, so you might happen upon young Xhosa initiates who are undergoing this age-old manhood ceremony.

Off-the-bike entertainment

The Wild Coast countryside is crammed with an incredible array of activities ranging from laid-back leisure and cultural options to wall-to-wall action. If you're the outdoor type, opt for one of a number of magnificent coastal hikes or saddle up for the multi-day Amadiba horse trail.

Snorkelling and diving are unmatched along the reefs and wrecks of Pondoland, while anglers agree that there is no better place in the world to bag a big fish.

Those in search of adrenalin may explore the Mzimvubu by canoe, 4x4 or quad bike into the rugged interior or sea kayak along the magnificent coastline.

Phenomenal birding, game viewing and hiking are the order of the day in nature reserves like Silaka, Hluleka, Dwesa, Cwebe and Mkambathi.

The culture and crafts of the amaXhosa are sure to captivate visitors to the area, and a visit to Qunu, the birthplace of Nelson Mandela, is a pilgrimage more and more people are making.

Also check out the Oliver Tambo Craft and Marketing Centre in Port St Johns, a community project where anything from imbo baskets to long-stemmed pipes changes hands.

OPPOSITE: Dramatic cliffs, pristine beaches and pockets of indigenous forest make the Wild Coast a must.

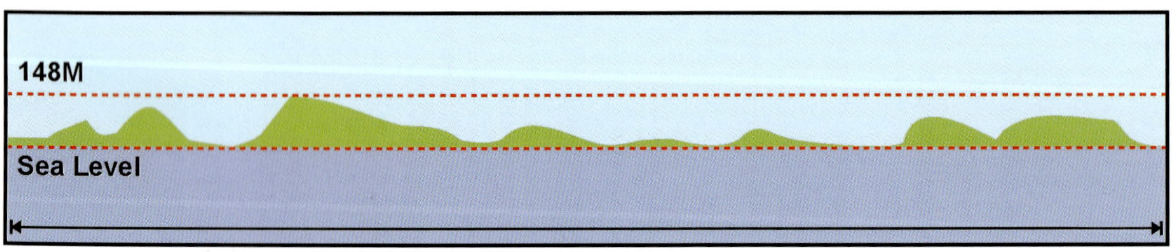

FAST FACTS

ROUTE
A linear route generally following the coast southwards from Hluleka to Coffee Bay.

TRAFFIC
Cows, goats, fishermen, flocks of oystercatchers, hikers, gaggles of ululating Xhosa kids.

ATTRACTIONS
Fairytale forests; end-of-the-earth cliffs; dreamy beaches; sweet singletrack; Transkei Gold.

START POINT
Hluleka Main Camp:
31°49.453' South, 29°18.147' East

FACILITIES
There are many private resorts, nature reserves, camp sites, backpackers, self-catering cottages, guesthouses and hotels along the Wild Coast.

ENTRY FEE
Gate fees are payable at Hluleka and other nature reserves, but the rest of the ride is for free.

CONTACT NUMBERS
Eastern Cape Tourism Board: (043) 701-9600
info@ectourism.co.za
www.ectourism.co.za
Map info: Craig Beech at cbeech@mighty.co.za

BEWARE OF
River crossings, sharks in estuaries, ticks, theft... you'll survive though.

THUMBS DOWN
No demarcated trail means you have to be adept at route finding, often along challenging terrain. Calculated risk, to some extent at least, is the name of the game along a ride certainly more suited to riders with a well-developed sense of adventure.

GLOSSARY

babyheads Roundish rocks that are often found in a loose jumble on hairpin corners or other dificult-to-negotiate sections of trail. Similar to death cookies, but bigger.

baobab Huge 'upside-down' trees found in the northern parts of South Africa and further north in Africa.

bomb To ride with wild disregard to personal safety.

bonk To run out of energy or grow exhausted on a ride.

bundu-bash To go where there is no road or track of any kind. This could happen if you get lost. If done deliberately, and on a consistent basis, vegetation is destroyed, and unsightly erosion is the outcome.

bunny hop To lift both wheels off the ground by crouching down and then exploding upward, pulling the bike with you. Useful for clearing obstructions, such as curbs, potholes and logs.

death cookies Fist-sized rocks that roll your bike in every direction but the one in which you want to go.

donga A steep-sided gully created by soil erosion.

endo The manoeuvre of flying unexpectedly over the handlebars, thus being forcibly ejected from the bike. Short for 'end over end'.

hard-pack An unsealed surface of compacted dried mud or soil or sand and rock. Normally quite smooth.

jeep track A very rough off-road track used by 4x4 vehicles. In essence it is two single tracks running parallel to each other. Not quite as rough as a singletrack, due to the fact that it carries vehicle traffic, but normally too rough for a normal motor vehicle.

kloof A mountain pass or gorge.

koppie A prominent, often isolated hill.

krans A sheer rock face.

mampoer A strong spirit distilled from wild fruit.

mopane An indigenous tree that produces very hard wood. Also called ironwood.

off-road Any track in the bush that is not a road in the traditional sense.

singletrack A narrow track just wide enough to be ridden or walked on by one person. Normally a rough path through the bush.

veld 'The bush', or open areas of natural vegetation.

OPPOSITE: Cycling Mecca: Cape Town riders shortcut through the Bo-Kaap to hit the slopes of Table Mountain.

AUTHORS' ACKNOWLEDGEMENTS

Any book is a team effort, and a great many friends, acquaintances and associates contributed to the glossy publication you now hold in your hands. Omnico, who sponsored my magic GT i-Drive, made every ride a pleasure. Garmin's e-trex Legend helped me map the trails. And welcoming landowners and local communities once again proved to me how fortunate I am to be a South African.

Many thanks to the design and editorial team at Struik (Alison Day and Erika Bornman) and also to the many moegoes who went riding with me – love your work!

And finally – to my daughter Beth – can't wait for you to grow up so you can come riding with me...

Jacques Marais

Thanks to all the landowners and relevant managers who, with their hospitality and assistance, provided not only access to the trails, but valuable insight as well. Special thanks to the rangers in the Kruger National Park who prevented us from being eaten by wild animals (thanks, Hein).

Thanks also to all my riding buddies, who acted as models, props, stunt riders and packhorses carrying cameras, GPSs, and camping gear around various trails around South Africa. Thanks Martin, Ettienne, Michael, Gordon, Chris, Nicolene, Robby (Mr Schwinn) and all the MAMBA folks who provided guides and riders for the photos.

Most of all, thanks to my wife, Susanna, who had to hold up the admin and domestic side of things. She compiled all my raw information into something useable while I was off riding cool trails and having fun. Without your help and support this would not have been possible.

Lastly, thanks to Struik for publishing this book, thereby making an investment in the sport we all love so much!

Herman Mills

To Craig Beech, our mapping technology knight in shining armour, who smartly turned around twenty maps in just four weeks: we trust this is an opportunity that will give you the recognition you truly deserve. Thanks, Craig, for illustrating 'the ride' aspect of this lovely book with such virtual clarity.

Susanna Mills

OPPOSITE: A view of the Gariep River from the peaks above the De Hoop camp site in the Richtersveld.

AUTHORS' INFO

Jacques Marais is a professional photographer and writer who freelances regularly for a range of South African publications, including *Men's Health, Sports Illustrated, Far Out, Expressions, Wegbreek* and *Out There Adventure Guide*. He is also a contributing editor to *Bicycling SA* magazine and his work occasionally appears in international publications such as *Quicksilver, Travesias* and *Open Skies*. Previous books include titles for both Struik and New Holland Publishing, covering outdoor survival, hiking and adventure racing.

As a confirmed trav-a-holic, Jacques enjoys exploring the furthest corners of the planet. Africa remains his favourite destination, however, and (when it comes to mountain biking) a touring ride along Ghana's Gold Coast to the Côte d'Ivoire stands out as a memorable adventure. If he had only one day of riding left, he'd spend it cruising cattle tracks along the Wild Coast.

More than a decade has passed since the love-at-first-sight mountain bike event where **Herman and Susanna Mills** first met. Although their careers are very different – Herman is a successful CRM solutions architect in the IT industry, while Susanna has worked as an art director in the advertising industry, and a freelance illustrator and designer – they share an enduring passion for mountain biking. They have co-authored two other books on the subject: *The Gary Fisher RSA MTB Trails Guidebook* in 1999 and *Adventure Sports: Mountain Biking* in 2000.

The Mills duo established the successful *Ride* magazine in 1997 – and for three years Herman acted as technical editor and Susanna as editor. They have also initiated and promoted several well-established off-road bicycle events together, including Rhodes, Koranna, Urban Assault, the Logwood Classic and the Barberton Classic.

Craig Beech is a keen cartographer and a passionate mountain biker. His trail maps were a highlight at the riders' briefings each evening during Cape Epic 2004. Look out for an extensive range of MTB trail maps from him in the future; some are already available through Willie Engelbrecht Cycles.

OPPOSITE: Sunset at the Augrabies National Park in the Northern Cape.

INDEX TO PLACES

Page references in *italics* indicate maps and photographs.

N

T

U

V

W

Y

Z

ABOVE: Heat, dust and dreams: sunset brings relief on the hottest ride.